MARK EXPLAINED

MARK EXPLAINED
Understanding the Book and Its Message for Today

Samuel Whitaker

Part of the Bible for Modern Life Series

Ascent Press

Published by
Ascent Press

ISBN: 978-1-972885-00-0

Printed in the United States of America

First Edition 2026

For those seeking clarity in the ancient words of Scripture.

CONTENTS

Disclaimer

This book provides an interpretive overview of the biblical text using historical scholarship and modern analysis tools. It is intended to help readers understand the themes, context, and message of the biblical narrative and is not intended to replace personal study of Scripture

Introduction

Why Mark Still Matters

Of the four Gospels, Mark is the one that wastes no time. Where Matthew opens with a genealogy and Luke with a carefully composed prologue, Mark begins mid-action: a voice in the wilderness, a river, a man rising from the water, and then movement — relentless, forward, urgent. There is no birth story, no magi, no angels singing over a manger. There is only the announcement that something has begun and the narrative that immediately demonstrates it. The shortest of the four Gospels is also its most propulsive, and that quality of motion is not accidental. It is the form that carries the argument.

Mark's Gospel covers the ministry, death, and resurrection of Jesus in sixteen compressed chapters. It records fewer of his extended teachings than any other Gospel. What it preserves instead is action: healings, exorcisms, confrontations, sea crossings, controversies, and an intensifying journey toward a cross that the reader sees coming long before the characters do. The narrative technique is distinctive — episodes placed inside other episodes, stories that illuminate each other by proximity, a sustained pattern of misunderstanding among the very people closest to Jesus. And then an ending that refuses to end, leaving the reader in the same silence and bewilderment as the women who fled from the empty tomb.

For readers who come to Mark expecting familiar Gospel territory, the experience can be disorienting. The Jesus of Mark is not primarily a teacher to be admired or a comforting presence to be sought. He is a figure of extraordinary and often unsettling authority — healing the sick, commanding unclean spirits, silencing storms, raising the dead, and all the while pressing his disciples toward a destination they neither understand nor welcome. He is emotionally vivid in ways the other Gospels sometimes soften: he sighs, he is moved, he is indignant, he is angry. He sleeps through storms. He is, in some ways, the most immediate and least domesticated Jesus in the New Testament.

That immediacy is the entry point this book attempts to open. Reading Mark well requires more than encountering its individual episodes. It requires understanding the world that shaped it, the structure that organizes it, the themes that run through it from announcement to empty tomb, and the specific demands it makes of readers who are willing to receive it on its own terms. The chapters that follow provide that orientation — not as a substitute for reading the Gospel itself but as preparation for reading it with the understanding it deserves.

Mark was not written for scholars. It was written for communities under pressure, people for whom the cost of following Jesus was becoming concrete and specific, and who needed a portrait of Jesus that was honest about what that cost meant and why it was worth paying. Those communities are not confined to the first century. The pressure takes different forms in different eras, but the human situation Mark addresses has not changed, and the portrait it offers continues to press its demands with the same urgency it brought to its first audience.

Chapter 1

The Human Question

*"The time has come. The kingdom of God has come near. Repent
and believe the good news."*
— Mark 1:15 (NIV)

The Universal Search for Meaning

Every human life is organized around some account of what
matters. The specific content of that account shifts across cultures
and centuries, but the underlying structure is consistent: people
need to know what is worth their time, their loyalty, their sacrifice.
They need to locate themselves within a story large enough to
make sense of their experience — the suffering, the aspiration, the
recognition that things are not as they should be, and that
something more is possible. These needs are not products of
particular religious traditions. They are features of human
consciousness as such, present in every culture that has ever
existed and persistent across every form of social change that
history has produced.

The Gospel of Mark addresses these needs not through
philosophical argument or systematic doctrine but through the
concentrated narration of a life. It presents a figure — Jesus of
Nazareth — as the one whose presence, teaching, death, and
resurrection constitute the most compelling and most
comprehensive answer available to the questions that human life
consistently generates. The presentation is not gentle or gradual.
Mark does not ease the reader into its claims. It opens with an
announcement — the kingdom of God has come near — and

builds from there with a momentum that does not pause for comfort or deliberation.

To understand why Mark makes its case this way requires attending to the situation of the people for whom it was first written. These were not comfortable inquirers approaching the Gospel from a position of safety and leisure. They were communities navigating genuine danger — Roman persecution, the social cost of religious commitment, the specific vulnerability of people who had attached their identity and their hope to a figure who had been publicly executed. They did not need a meditation on abstract questions. They needed to know whether the one they had followed was who the story claimed him to be, whether the suffering they were experiencing was the kind of suffering that had meaning, and whether the kingdom he had announced was real enough to organize a life around in conditions that made organizing any life at all a daily act of courage.

What distinguishes Mark's approach to these questions is a quality of compressed insistence. Where Matthew's Gospel circles back repeatedly to explore dimensions of Jesus' teaching, and Luke's expands into social commentary and careful literary arrangement, Mark drives straight ahead. The repeated word that characterizes its narrative — *immediately* — is both a stylistic trait and a theological claim. Things happen now in Mark. The call goes out, and the nets are dropped before the sentence ends. The unclean spirit is confronted and expelled before the crowd has finished being astonished. The world the Gospel describes is one in which the arrival of genuine authority leaves no room for extended deliberation.

This quality of urgency is not simply an ancient cultural texture that modern readers must acknowledge and set aside. It is the natural form of a narrative about something genuinely unprecedented — about a presence that enters the human situation and changes it, not through gradual persuasion but through direct and immediate action. The questions that Mark's audience was asking were not academic. They were the questions of people whose lives were already in motion, already shaped by commitment to something that was costing them dearly, already pressed toward the center of what the Gospel claims. Reading Mark well means allowing that urgency to function rather than managing it from a comfortable distance.

The Pressure of Genuine Need

The people who move through Mark's Gospel are not, for the most part, philosophically curious. They are desperate. A man with an unclean spirit cries out in the synagogue. A woman with a hemorrhage pushes through a crowd just to touch the hem of Jesus' garment, having spent everything she had on physicians who could not help her. A father whose daughter is dying throws himself at Jesus' feet with a request that sounds less like a prayer than a declaration of last resort. A blind man shouts from the roadside with a persistence that embarrasses the disciples around him. These are people at the edge of what their frameworks for managing life can contain, and their movement toward Jesus is not primarily theological. It is the movement of genuine, unmanageable need toward the only source of help that appears adequate to it.

This dimension of Mark deserves careful attention because it establishes the register in which the Gospel is operating. The kingdom of God that Jesus announces is not, in Mark's presentation, a spiritual framework that enables better management of ordinary life. It is the arrival of something that addresses what ordinary life, left to its own resources, cannot address — the powers that diminish and destroy human existence, the forces that hold people captive, the conditions of exclusion and loss and death that constitute the outer boundary of what the world as it currently operates can do to a human being. Mark's Jesus meets people at that boundary, and his ministry is defined by the consistent movement of divine authority toward precisely the conditions that human authority has consistently failed to remedy.

For modern readers in societies with sophisticated medical and psychological resources, the rawness of Mark's depictions of need can initially seem remote — a feature of an ancient world that has been largely superseded. But the needs that appear in Mark are not abolished by technology or therapy. The sense of being held captive by something one cannot name, the experience of having exhausted the frameworks available for addressing a fundamental problem and finding them inadequate, the desperation that accompanies genuine loss — these are not exclusively ancient experiences. They are features of the human condition that persist regardless of the century or the sophistication of the culture in which they appear. Mark's Gospel speaks to these conditions with unusual directness precisely because it does not pretend they can be managed at the level at which they actually present themselves.

The Question of Authority

No theme surfaces more consistently in Mark's opening chapters than the question of where genuine authority comes from. The crowds in the Capernaum synagogue are astonished not simply at what Jesus says but at the mode of his saying it — he teaches *as one who has authority*, not as the scribes. The scribes are not incompetent. They are the trained interpreters of the most important documents their society possesses, and their interpretation has shaped communal life across generations. But their authority is derivative. It borrows its standing from the tradition they have mastered. Jesus does not operate within that framework. He speaks in his own name, from a source of standing that the tradition has not provided and cannot evaluate.

This distinction matters enormously for what follows, because everything Mark presents about Jesus flows from the claim that his authority is genuinely different in kind from the authority that human structures and institutions generate. It is not the authority of mastery, expertise, or office. It is the authority that commands even the unclean spirits and is obeyed — the authority that the forces holding human beings captive recognize and cannot resist. The crowds who observe this are not simply impressed. They are confronting something for which they have no adequate category, and their astonishment is the appropriate response to a genuine rupture in the expected order of things.

The question of authority is not merely a first-century problem. It is one of the most consistently pressing questions of any era, including the present one. Authority is eroding across every domain — political, religious, institutional, professional — and the erosion is, in many cases, deserved, the consequence of authority exercised for the benefit of those who held it rather than those it was supposed to serve. The hunger for genuine authority — for someone or something that can be trusted to do what it claims, whose standing does not depend on the willingness of others to extend credit — is everywhere evident precisely because the supply is so thin. Mark presents a figure whose authority is not borrowed, not institutional, not conditional on human recognition. It is demonstrated, repeatedly and systematically, in the healing and liberation of the people from whom life has been taken.

The Longing for Genuine Deliverance

Mark's Gospel also engages a specifically Jewish longing that runs beneath the surface of every encounter it describes — the expectation, shaped by centuries of prophetic and apocalyptic promise, that God would act decisively to overthrow the powers that held his people captive. This was not a longing for private spiritual comfort. It was a corporate hope for concrete deliverance — for the end of occupation, the restoration of dignity, and the arrival of a new order in which the powers that currently governed the world would be displaced by the reign of God.

Mark presents Jesus as the one in whom this corporate longing finds its unexpected and disorienting fulfillment. The announcement that opens his public ministry — the time has come, the kingdom of God has come near — is not a gentle invitation to spiritual reflection. It is a declaration that the moment the tradition had been moving toward has arrived, and that the appropriate response is not deliberation but repentance and belief. But the fulfillment arrives in forms that repeatedly confound the expectations of those who most longed for it. The disciples who follow Jesus most closely misunderstand him most consistently. The messianic identity he carries is not proclaimed but concealed. The fulfillment of Israel's hope comes through a cross, not a conquest, and the disciples are not prepared for this even after they have been told it will happen.

The longing for genuine deliverance — for a different order of things than what the present moment offers, for the actual resolution of what is broken rather than its management — is not exclusive to first-century Judaism. It is a feature of human experience across every cultural context and every historical period. What Mark's engagement with Jewish apocalyptic hope offers to readers from every background is a window into the dynamics of expectation and its fulfillment that remain consistent regardless of the specific form the expectation takes. The pattern it reveals is this: genuine deliverance tends to arrive through means that the people who most longed for it were least prepared to accept, because the means of deliverance cannot be separated from the nature of what is being delivered from and the character of the one doing the delivering.

The Question of Power

Mark's Gospel is also deeply interested in what genuine power looks like and where it comes from. This is not a peripheral concern but a central one that shapes the entire first half of the narrative. The earliest chapters are dominated not by extended teaching but by demonstrations of authority over the forces that diminish and destroy human life — unclean spirits, disease, paralysis, storm, death itself. This concentration is not accidental. Mark is establishing the nature of the one he is describing before that nature is given its full theological articulation.

The pattern is consistent and deliberate. Jesus enters a synagogue and immediately encounters a man with an unclean spirit. He rebukes it, and it leaves. The crowd is astonished not at the content of his teaching but at the authority with which he acts. Teachers explain and interpret. They do not issue commands to the forces that hold human beings captive and have those commands obeyed. What the crowd witnesses in the Capernaum synagogue is not a more skilled version of the religious authority they are accustomed to. It is a different kind of authority entirely — one that operates directly rather than derivatively, that acts rather than argues, that produces immediate results in the lives of people from whom life has been taken.

The pattern of encounter and restoration that runs through Mark's early chapters — the possessed man in the synagogue, the fever-stricken woman, the leper, the paralytic — is sometimes read as a series of individual miracle stories with independent significance. But Mark's presentation is more sustained and more purposeful than that. These are not isolated demonstrations arranged for general edification. They are a cumulative portrait of a power that is recognizably consistent in its orientation: it moves toward suffering rather than away from it, it addresses what has diminished human beings rather than ignoring it, and it produces restoration rather than mere relief. This consistency is itself the argument Mark is making — not just that Jesus is powerful but that his power moves in a specific direction, toward specific people, for a specific purpose that will ultimately be fully revealed at the cross.

The Shape of What Follows

These dimensions — the urgency of human need, the nature of the authority that addresses it, the question of genuine power, and the longing for deliverance that finds its unexpected fulfillment — are not separate topics that Mark handles in separate places. They are angles on a single claim that the Gospel develops from its first verse to its last. The urgency of Mark's narrative is the formal expression of the urgency of the situation it describes: something has happened in the person of Jesus that cannot be received at a comfortable distance, and the response it requires is not eventual but immediate.

The chapters that follow examine the historical world that shaped Mark's perspective, the literary structure that organizes its argument, the major themes that recur throughout its narrative, the ways it has been misread, and the specific ways it continues to address the lives of people who encounter it seriously. The goal throughout is not to make Mark easier to receive but to make it possible to receive it more fully — to remove the obstacles that prevent modern readers from engaging the text as the sustained, demanding, pastorally serious document it is. Mark rewards the reader who brings honest attention to it. The chapters that follow are an attempt to equip that attention and to prepare readers for an encounter with a Gospel that does not wait for them to be ready before making its demands. It has never waited. It does not wait now.

Chapter 2

Orientation

"The beginning of the good news about Jesus the Messiah, the Son of God."
— Mark 1:1

A Gospel for a Community Under Pressure

The historical circumstances that produced Mark's Gospel are not background information to be noted and set aside. They are the living conditions that explain why the Gospel sounds the way it does — why its pace is relentless, why its portrait of Jesus is so physically immediate, why its treatment of suffering is so honest, why it ends the way it does rather than with the measured resolution that most narratives provide. Mark is a document shaped at every level by the pressure under which it was composed, and understanding that pressure is the first step toward understanding the Gospel itself.

Mark was almost certainly composed in the late 60s CE, making it the earliest of the four Gospels to be written. The community for which it was written was navigating one of the most dangerous periods in the early history of the Jesus movement. The most plausible location is Rome, where followers of Jesus had experienced or were anticipating systematic persecution under Nero following the great fire of 64 CE. The Neronian persecution was not abstract religious tension. It was arrests, executions, and the use of Christians as scapegoats for a disaster they did not cause. People who identified publicly with Jesus were at risk, and the question of what faithful endurance looked like under genuine threat was not theoretical. It was the question their lives were organized around.

This context illuminates Mark's distinctive treatment of suffering in ways that careful reading makes visible. The disciples who fail and flee in the passion narrative are not included as cautionary tales about poor discipleship. They are mirrors in which communities under pressure could recognize their own experience — the gap between intention and capacity when the cost of commitment becomes concrete and immediate. The crowds who follow Jesus enthusiastically through Galilee and then fall away are recognizable to anyone who has watched people respond to a call with genuine initial enthusiasm and then encounter the specific conditions under which that call must be lived. Mark is writing for people who have already discovered what following Jesus costs, and the Gospel they receive does not pretend the cost is manageable if only one's faith is strong enough. It tells the truth about failure and offers something more sustaining than idealization would have provided.

The Roman context, if accurate, also gives Mark's sustained attention to the question of power its specific gravity. Communities living under Roman imperial authority knew exactly what worldly power looked like at its most sophisticated and its most ruthless. Mark's portrait of a Jesus who exercises a fundamentally different kind of power — consistently oriented toward the restoration of those from whom life has been taken, rather than toward the domination of those who threaten the powerful — was not a generic spiritual claim. It was a direct counter-testimony to the most visible claim to ultimate authority in the known world. The assertion that the crucified Jesus is the Son of God was not only a theological affirmation. It was a declaration about where genuine sovereignty resided in a world in which the title *Son of God* was regularly claimed by the emperor.

Who Wrote Mark and When

The Gospel does not identify its author within the text. The attribution to Mark is traditional, drawn from the testimony of Papias of Hierapolis in the early second century, who describes the author as Peter's interpreter — someone who recorded Peter's teaching with accuracy, though not in narrative sequence. The figure traditionally identified is John Mark, a companion of Paul and Barnabas who appears in Acts and in several Pauline letters. The tradition connecting the Gospel to Peter's preaching circles is early enough to carry weight, even if it cannot be independently verified by other means.

What internal evidence establishes is that the author was writing for an audience that included readers unfamiliar with Jewish customs — he explains practices that a Jewish audience would not have needed explained — and that the Greek of the Gospel is the most colloquial and least polished of the four. Neither of these features represents a deficiency. They represent deliberate choices of accessibility over elegance, clarity over literary refinement. The author's concern is not to impress readers with sophisticated Greek prose but to communicate with people for whom the story of Jesus was new or partially understood and for whom the primary need was not literary pleasure but pastoral sustenance.

Most scholars place the composition between 65 and 70 CE. The primary evidence is the relative simplicity of the Gospel's theological development compared to Matthew and Luke, the absence of any clear reference to the destruction of Jerusalem as a past event, and the tradition connecting the text to Peter, whose death under Nero would place the composition in the mid-to-late 60s. The urgency that characterizes every page of the Gospel fits a community for whom the question of faithful endurance under genuine pressure was not a future consideration but an immediate demand that shaped every decision of daily life.

The Structure of the Gospel

Mark is organized around a geographical and theological hinge. The first half — chapters 1 through 8 — takes place in and around Galilee and is dominated by the question of who Jesus is. The reader is given the answer in the Gospel's first verse: the Son of God. But the human characters in the narrative spend eight chapters failing to understand what the reader already knows, and the gap between the reader's knowledge and the characters' incomprehension generates a sustained dramatic tension that does not fully resolve until a Roman soldier — the last person anyone would expect — looks at the dying Jesus and says the only adequate thing: *Surely this man was the Son of God.*

The second half — chapters 8 through 16 — pivots on Peter's confession at Caesarea Philippi and moves steadily toward Jerusalem, the cross, and the empty tomb. Three times, Jesus predicts his suffering, death, and resurrection. Three times, the disciples demonstrate that they have not understood what he is telling them. The journey is not merely geographical. It is a sustained theological argument pressed from three different angles, because the resistance the argument is working against is deep and persistent and cannot be dislodged by a single statement made once at a single moment.

Within this two-part structure, Mark employs several distinctive literary techniques. The most characteristic is intercalation — sometimes called the Markan sandwich — in which one story is placed inside another so that each illuminates the other. The cleansing of the Temple is placed inside the account of the cursing and withering of the fig tree. The healing of the hemorrhaging woman is placed inside the raising of Jairus's daughter. In each case the meaning of the outer story and the meaning of the inner story are mutually interpretive in ways that neither would yield in isolation. Mark also structures his material through repetition and pairing: two feeding miracles, two blind men healed, two accounts of disciples failing to understand after a sea crossing. The pairings are not accidental narrative redundancy. They are interpretive devices that invite comparison and accumulate significance as the narrative progresses.

Mark's Sources

Mark does not appear to have composed his Gospel without reference to earlier material. The two-source hypothesis that accounts for the literary relationships among the Synoptic Gospels identifies Mark as the earliest Gospel and the primary narrative source for both Matthew and Luke. The evidence for this — called Markan priority — is substantial: Matthew and Luke consistently follow Mark's narrative sequence, their versions of shared material tend to be more polished than Mark's, and they independently smooth out features of Mark that might have seemed theologically or stylistically awkward to their respective audiences.

What this means is that Mark was not simply transcribing what he received. He was selecting, arranging, and interpreting earlier material in light of the pastoral needs of a specific community and the theological argument he was making. The passion narrative in particular shows signs of being the most developed and coherent unit in the Gospel, suggesting that the story of Jesus' death had been told and retold in community contexts before Mark organized it as the extended climax of his account. Reading Mark well means reading it as a crafted argument, not simply as a collection of preserved memories whose arrangement was determined by the order in which they happened to be recalled.

Mark's Portrait of Jesus

The Christological portrait Mark develops is constructed through the accumulation of titles and demonstration across sixteen chapters. Jesus is the Son of God — announced in verse one, confirmed at the baptism, recognized by the unclean spirits before any human character understands it, and confessed at the cross by the centurion. He is the Messiah — the title Peter uses at Caesarea Philippi, the hinge of the entire narrative. He is the Son of Man — the designation Jesus uses most consistently in his own speech, drawn from Daniel's vision of cosmic authority, combining the humility of present suffering with the glory of future coming in a single title that prevents either from being isolated from the other.

Alongside these titles, Mark preserves a portrait of Jesus that is unusually physical and emotionally specific. He grows weary. He is moved with compassion. He is indignant. He sighs deeply. He sleeps in the stern of a boat through a storm. These details are not humanizing ornaments added to soften a distant theological figure. They are constitutive of the portrait Mark is painting — a portrait in which the full embodied reality of Jesus is as much a part of the theological claim as his authority over wind and waves. The Gospel insists that both dimensions belong to the same person and that the full portrait requires holding both without collapsing either dimension into the other.

The Role of the Disciples

No dimension of Mark is more immediately striking to careful readers than its portrait of the disciples. They misunderstand Jesus with a consistency and completeness that the other Gospels do not match. They argue about who is greatest immediately after a passion prediction. They fall asleep in Gethsemane. They flee at the arrest. Peter denies Jesus three times. The women who come to the tomb in the end flee in silence. The portrait is honest to the point of discomfort, and the discomfort is theologically deliberate.

The disciples cannot fully understand Jesus before the cross and resurrection because those events are what makes genuine understanding possible. Their failure is not a narrative embarrassment to be explained away. It is a feature that Mark has preserved and emphasized because it serves the central argument the Gospel is making: that the identity of Jesus can only be truly grasped when it is grasped in light of the cross, and that any portrait of discipleship that does not include the full reality of failure is not honest about what following Jesus actually involves in the real world under real conditions.

The Ending of Mark

No feature of the Gospel has generated more sustained discussion than its ending. The earliest and most reliable manuscripts end at 16:8, with the women fleeing from the empty tomb because they were afraid. The longer ending that appears in many manuscript traditions is widely recognized by scholars as a later addition, composed to bring Mark into conformity with the resurrection appearances narrated in the other Gospels and to provide the resolution that the original ending withholds.

The original ending is deliberately open. It withholds the comfort of resolution. The women have received the most significant news in human history, and they flee from it in silence. The disciples have been told where the risen Jesus is going, but the response to that news has not been made within the narrative. The reader is left in the same position as the women, with the evidence of resurrection before them and the question of what to do with it still pressing and unanswered. This is not a deficiency. It is the most honest ending the story could have, and the most demanding: the Gospel that has pressed urgency from its first word presses it one final time, at the moment of greatest significance, and waits to see what the reader will do.

Preparing to Read Mark Well

Understanding the historical context of Mark's composition, the community for which it was written, the sources the author drew upon, the structural features that organize its argument, the portrait of Jesus developed through title and demonstration, the role of the disciples as theological argument rather than simple characterization, and the significance of the Gospel's deliberately open ending: all of these are forms of orientation that prepare the reader to engage the text itself more fully.

But orientation is preparation, not replacement. The goal of everything this chapter has described is to remove the obstacles that can prevent a modern reader from engaging Mark directly — the sense that its abruptness is a deficiency, that its rough edges are imprecision, that its unresolved ending is incompleteness. When those obstacles are cleared, what remains is the text itself: a concentrated, urgent, pastorally honest, theologically serious engagement with the question of who Jesus is and what following him requires when the cost of following is real.

Mark rewards the reader who brings sustained, attentive, honest engagement. Its brevity is deceptive — there is more happening in its sixteen chapters than any single reading can fully draw out. The reader who returns to it repeatedly, who allows the second half to reframe the first, who brings the experience of their own failure and fear to a text that has always known about failure and fear, will consistently find that Mark has more to say than any previous reading has fully exhausted. The orientation this chapter provides is the beginning of that engagement, not its completion.

Chapter 3

The World Behind the Book

*"At that time Jesus came from Nazareth in Galilee and was
baptized by John in the Jordan."*
— *Mark 1:9*

Roman Galilee and the World Jesus Inhabited

The world that produced Mark's narrative was shaped by two
forces whose intersection was both generative and explosive:
Roman imperial power and Jewish religious life. Rome provided
the administrative structure — taxation, military presence, legal
authority, the infrastructure of roads and commerce that
connected the Mediterranean world. But for the Jewish population
of Galilee and Judea, the more immediate context was the Torah,
the synagogue, and the memory of the Temple. These were not
competing frameworks that could be easily held at a distance from
each other. They met in every aspect of daily life, and the pressure
their collision generated was a defining feature of the world Jesus
moved through.

Galilee, where the majority of Mark's action takes place, had a
character distinct from Judea. It was predominantly rural, more
ethnically mixed, more remote from the centers of religious
authority concentrated in Jerusalem. Herod Antipas, who ruled as
Rome's client during Jesus' ministry, had built his capital of
Tiberias on the western shore of the Sea of Galilee — a
Hellenistic city constructed on a burial site, ritually impure and
therefore avoided by observant Jews. The proximity of this
symbol of Roman-sponsored cultural imperialism to the villages
and fishing communities where Jesus ministered created a

constant visible reminder of the pressure that imperial culture was exerting on communities trying to maintain their distinctive covenant identity against the forces pressing in from every side.

Rome generally tolerated subject religions that did not threaten public order, but the toleration was always conditional and always provisional. The question of taxation was a persistent and specific point of tension — not only because of its economic burden on a largely agricultural population operating near subsistence level, but because the coins used to pay it bore the emperor's image and the inscriptions that claimed divine status for him. For Jews who took the first commandment seriously, participating in an economy structured around that coinage was itself a form of complicity that their convictions made deeply uncomfortable. When Jesus is asked about paying taxes to Caesar in Mark's twelfth chapter, the question is not hypothetical. It carries the full weight of a debate that had shaped Jewish life under Roman occupation for generations and that had real consequences for those who answered it one way or another.

The Economic Landscape

The economic conditions of first-century Galilee are directly relevant to Mark's narrative in ways that are easy to underestimate if the text is read without this context. Taxation was layered and cumulative — Roman taxes on land and produce, Herodian tolls and levies, Temple tax and agricultural tithes required by Torah, all pressing simultaneously on a population whose subsistence margins were already thin. Fishermen working the Sea of Galilee were subject not only to these general obligations but to toll leases through which Roman authorities extracted fees from the fishing industry itself. The catch pulled from the water was subject to imperial extraction at the point of landing.

When Jesus calls Simon and Andrew beside the Sea of Galilee, and they leave their nets immediately, the narrative is not describing romantic figures free from material constraint. It is describing working men operating within an economic system that made vulnerability a constant feature of life at every level below the social elite. Their immediate response to the call is not the product of unusual spiritual sensitivity. It is the response of people who have encountered something so evidently real that the economic framework organizing their daily existence is suddenly visible for what it is — not the boundary of possibility but a context that can be left behind when something more genuinely authoritative arrives.

The crowds of sick and marginalized people who gather around Jesus throughout Mark are not background scenery. They are, in many cases, the people whom the economic and social system has pushed to its outer edges — those whose conditions made it impossible to maintain the combination of economic productivity and ritual purity that participation in ordinary community life required. The lepers, the hemorrhaging woman, the blind beggars, the man living among the tombs — these are people the system has expelled. Mark's Jesus moves consistently toward them, and this directional consistency is not incidental to the Gospel's theological argument. It is the argument in visible form.

The World of the Synagogue

By the first century, the synagogue had become the primary institution of Jewish communal life outside Jerusalem — a place of Torah reading and interpretation, prayer, community gathering, and the formation of communal identity week by week. The scribes who appear throughout Mark's Gospel were the recognized authorities in this setting, the trained interpreters whose expertise gave them significant social and religious standing in every community where they served.

Jesus is repeatedly presented as teaching in the synagogues of Galilee, and the conflict that develops between him and the scribal tradition is shaped by this shared institutional context. When the crowd in the Capernaum synagogue responds to Jesus' teaching with astonishment — *he teaches as one having authority, not as the scribes* — they are not simply noting a difference in rhetorical style or personal confidence. They are recognizing a difference in the nature of the standing being claimed. The scribes' authority derived from the chain of interpretation that connected their teaching to the received tradition. Jesus' authority does not borrow its standing from precedent. It speaks from a source the tradition has not generated and cannot adjudicate, and the crowd recognizes the difference immediately.

The tension between Jesus and the scribal tradition in Mark is not simply an intellectual dispute about the correct interpretation of particular texts. It is a conflict about the nature and source of religious authority in a community whose entire identity was organized around a body of sacred texts and their authorized interpretation. When scribes come from Jerusalem to investigate Jesus and conclude that he casts out demons by the power of Beelzebul, they are not engaging in open theological inquiry. They are making an official determination designed to delegitimize a figure whose authority they cannot accommodate within their framework and therefore must neutralize by attributing it to the most malevolent possible source.

The Scribes and Their World

The scribes in Mark's Gospel are frequently read through the lens of the controversy narratives, producing a caricature of rigid, self-serving religious professionals whose primary concern was the protection of their institutional standing. This caricature is historically inaccurate and theologically unhelpful. The scribal tradition represented a genuine intellectual achievement that had made the covenant community possible across centuries of disruption and exile. The scribes were the guardians of a body of interpretation without which the Torah could not have functioned as a living guide for community life in the changed circumstances of each successive generation.

The problem Mark's Jesus identifies with the scribal tradition is not cynicism or corruption in the simple sense. It is something more structural and, in some ways, more tragic: the tendency of a highly developed system of textual authority to become self-referential, generating its own internal standards of legitimacy that gradually substitute for the direct encounter with the living God to whom the texts were always pointing. When the scribes evaluate Jesus by asking what tradition authorizes his actions and find no satisfactory answer within their framework, they are not simply being obstructionist. They are applying the only evaluative criteria their formation has given them to a phenomenon their formation did not prepare them to recognize. The tragedy is not that the criteria are corrupt. It is that they are insufficient for what they are being asked to evaluate, and the insufficiency is built into the structure of derived authority itself.

Messianic Expectation in First-Century Judaism

The first century was a period of intense and varied messianic expectation. The combination of Roman occupation, economic pressure, and the accumulated weight of prophetic promise had created a climate in which hope for divine intervention was not merely a theological category but a social force shaping concrete political choices and everyday patterns of life. Different groups within Judaism held different versions of this hope — some centered on military deliverance, others on priestly renewal, others on the apocalyptic transformation of the entire cosmic order.

Mark presents a Messiah who engages all of these expectations and is reducible to none of them. The path from the

opening announcement — the kingdom of God has come near —
to the centurion's confession at the cross runs directly through
suffering, rejection, and death, a path that no available version of
messianic expectation had mapped in advance. The distance
between expectation and fulfillment is one of Mark's central
subjects. The disciples' repeated failure to understand the passion
predictions is not obtuseness. It is the natural response of people
whose entire framework for understanding messiahship has been
constructed around categories that the actual Messiah's path
consistently transcends and finally redefines.

The Experience of Exile and Restoration

Beneath the surface of Mark's narrative runs the longer story of
Israel's experience of exile and incomplete restoration. The return
from Babylon had not produced the full renewal the prophets had
announced. The Temple had been rebuilt, but the Davidic
monarchy had not been restored, and the nation remained subject
to foreign powers. Many first-century Jews understood themselves
as still living in a kind of extended exile — the conditions the
prophets had associated with full restoration had not yet
materialized, and the sense of suspended promise gave particular
urgency to texts that spoke of its definitive end.

Mark places this entire framework at the beginning of his
Gospel by opening with a quotation from Malachi and Isaiah
about a voice crying in the wilderness and a way being prepared
for the Lord. John the Baptist is the messenger. Jesus is the Lord
whose way is being prepared. The baptism that follows is not
merely a personal religious experience. The heavens are *torn open*
— the same Greek word Mark uses later for the tearing of the
Temple curtain — and the Spirit descends and the voice speaks,
and what the prophets had announced as the beginning of Israel's
definitive restoration is presented as having arrived, in a form that
both fulfills and exceeds what the prophetic imagination had

anticipated. The exile is ending. The promised restoration is beginning. And it is beginning in a form that will require everything the disciples have to understand.

Daily Life, Household, and Social World

The social world of first-century Galilee was organized around the household — the extended family unit that served simultaneously as economic enterprise, educational institution, and primary context for religious formation. The values of honor and shame that governed public reputation across the Mediterranean world shaped every aspect of this social structure. Honor was not merely a psychological benefit but a practical social resource — essential to one's ability to function in economic, legal, and community relationships. Its absence or removal was not an emotional wound but a material catastrophe that affected every dimension of a person's ability to participate in ordinary community life.

This context illuminates the social dimension of Jesus' healings in Mark in ways that a purely medical reading misses. The leper who is cleansed is not simply relieved of physical suffering. He is restored to the social world from which his condition had entirely excluded him. The hemorrhaging woman is not simply healed of a physical condition. She is freed from twelve years of ritual impurity that had cut her off from full participation in community life and from all the relationships and economic activities that community participation made possible. The Gerasene demoniac is not simply delivered from a spiritual condition. He is returned from the tombs — the outer boundary of the human social world — to his family and community, restored to the network of relationships that constitute a human life. When Mark records that Jesus restored these people, he means something more comprehensive than medical intervention. He means the reconstitution of a person's entire social existence.

A World Defined by Urgency

The world behind Mark is finally a world in which urgency is not manufactured but earned — the urgency of communities under genuine pressure, of long-deferred hopes pressing toward resolution, of a political and social situation whose instability everyone could feel and whose consequences no one could fully predict. The prophets who had sustained Israel through previous crises had done so not by minimizing the difficulty of the present or offering comfortable assurances about the future, but by locating within the pressure itself the grounds for a response that circumstances alone could not generate.

Mark's Gospel inhabits this same urgency. It was written for communities that knew what pressure felt like — from Roman power, from economic vulnerability, from the specific challenge of living as a minority community in a culture that did not share its convictions. It does not offer easy comfort or quick resolution. It offers a Jesus who moves toward suffering rather than away from it, disciples who fail but are not finally abandoned, and an open future whose certainty rests not on present conditions but on the character of the one who has entered those conditions and demonstrated what his character means in the most difficult circumstances imaginable. This is the world behind the book — not a world of settled certainty but a world of tested urgency, sustained by the conviction that the one who tore open the heavens at the Jordan had not finished what he came to do.

The Death That Transformed the World

No feature of the world behind Mark is more historically significant or more theologically weighted than the fact of Roman crucifixion. The cross was not a neutral instrument of death in the first-century world. It was the specific technology by which Rome eliminated those who threatened public order and demonstrated to subject populations the absolute reach of imperial power. To be crucified was to die in public, slowly, stripped of dignity, with one's body displayed as a warning to any who might consider similar resistance. It was a death designed to humiliate as much as to kill, and the humiliation was part of the message Rome intended to send.

This context is essential to understanding why the claim that a crucified man was the Son of God carried the specific force it carried in the communities for which Mark was written. In the Roman world, the title *Son of God* belonged to the emperor. The emperor's power was legitimate, celebrated, and backed by the full force of the most sophisticated military and administrative apparatus the ancient world had produced. To transfer that title to a man who had been publicly executed by Roman authority was not merely a theological statement. It was a counterclaim about the nature of genuine power and the location of genuine sovereignty that carried real and specific danger for those who made it.

Mark was written into this context for communities who understood the risk the counterclaim involved. The Gospel's sustained argument that Jesus' crucifixion was not the defeat of his authority, but its fullest expression was not an abstract theological proposition. It was the claim that made it possible to keep following a crucified Messiah in a world that regarded his manner of death as the final word on his significance. Understanding this context does not reduce the theological claim to sociology. It clarifies why the claim needed to be made with the specific form of urgency and the specific kind of honesty that Mark brings to it.

Chapter 4

The Story or Flow of the Book

"He appointed twelve that they might be with him and that he might send them out to preach."
— Mark 3:14

The Shape of Mark's Narrative

Mark unfolds as a story with a destination. Every element of its structure — the compressed opening, the accumulating demonstrations of authority, the hinge of Peter's confession, the three-fold passion prediction cycle, the compressed passion narrative, and the deliberately open ending — serves the movement toward and through the cross. The narrative does not wander. It moves with a purposefulness that reflects the theological argument it is making: the story of Jesus is not a series of episodes with individual significance but a single sustained movement from announcement to cross to empty tomb, and the meaning of every part depends on its relationship to the whole.

The theological architecture of this movement is as important as its narrative momentum. Mark is not simply recording what happened. He is constructing an argument about who Jesus is and what following him requires, and the argument is embedded in the narrative structure itself — in what is placed next to what, in what is placed inside what, in what is repeated and in what pattern, in what is withheld from the characters while being available to the reader. Reading Mark as a sequence of individual episodes misses the argument that only the whole can carry, and misses the specific features of the whole that distinguish it from every other account of Jesus' ministry in the New Testament.

The two major phases of the narrative are joined at the geographical and theological hinge of Caesarea Philippi. The first phase establishes Jesus' identity through accumulated demonstration and confronts the consistent human failure to understand what is being demonstrated. The second phase defines what that identity costs and what genuine participation in the kingdom it inaugurates requires. Neither half is intelligible without the other. The identity established in the first gives the passion in the second its meaning. The passion in the second gives the identity established in the first its full content and its most demanding implication.

Announcement and Authority

The opening of Mark's Gospel is unlike any other beginning in ancient literature. It announces its subject — the good news about Jesus the Messiah, the Son of God — and then proceeds without further preparation directly into the narrative. John the Baptist appears in the wilderness. Crowds come from Jerusalem and Judea. Jesus arrives from Nazareth, is baptized, and the heavens are torn open. The Spirit descends. The voice speaks. Mark's opening moves at the speed of its own urgency, establishing the identity of Jesus through a combination of heavenly declaration and prophetic fulfillment before a single human character has said a word about who this person is.

The temptation narrative that follows is compressed to two verses — a striking contrast with Matthew's extended dialogue and Luke's detailed encounter. Jesus is driven into the wilderness, tested by Satan, attended by angels, and returns. The brevity is characteristic of Mark, but it is not emptiness. The wilderness imagery evokes the language of Israel's formation in the desert. The wild animals evoke prophetic visions of restored creation. The angels evoke divine provision in the tradition of the Exodus narrative. Mark is locating Jesus within Israel's story without narrating the connection explicitly, trusting its readers to recognize what the imagery is doing and to understand that the one who emerges from the wilderness is stepping into the fulfillment of a story that the wilderness itself has always been preparing for.

The call of the first disciples continues the compressed urgency of the opening. *Come, follow me.* The fishermen beside the Sea of Galilee leave their nets immediately. James and John leave not only their nets but their father. The narrative moves too quickly to supply psychological explanation, and the omission is not a gap but a claim: the authority of the call is sufficient to produce the response. The point is not the disciples' internal process but the nature of the one who calls and the adequacy of his authority to produce an immediate and total response that no other authority in the narrative world of the Gospel could have generated.

The Galilean Ministry

The first three chapters of the Galilean ministry establish the pattern that will govern everything that follows. Jesus teaches in the synagogue with authority. He encounters an unclean spirit and commands it. He heals Peter's mother-in-law. He cleanses a leper. He heals a paralytic and simultaneously pronounces the forgiveness of sins — a move that generates the first explicit controversy about who he is and what he is claiming for himself. The pattern is consistent and cumulative: authority is demonstrated, the scope of that authority expands with each episode, and the response of those who witness it ranges from astonishment to hostility depending on whether the witness is among those who are helped or among those whose frameworks are threatened.

The controversy narratives of chapter 2 introduce the formal opposition that will intensify through the Gospel. Each controversy is a variant on the same underlying question: by what authority does this man do what he is doing, and who gave him the right to do it? The scribes who question his authority to forgive sins, the Pharisees who question his table fellowship with sinners, the disciples of John who question his approach to fasting, the Pharisees who question his approach to Sabbath observance — each group is pressing the same question from a different angle. The accumulation of controversies is not random. It is a portrait of institutional resistance to a presence that the existing frameworks cannot accommodate, growing more organized and more determined as the demonstrations of authority become more comprehensive.

The Parable Discourse and the Hinge

The parable discourse of chapter 4 represents the most sustained block of teaching in the first half of Mark, and its placement — delivered from a boat pushed out into the water, with the crowd on the shore — creates a visual image of the distance between the teacher and the audience that the parables themselves develop thematically. The parable of the sower does not merely describe different kinds of receptivity. It invites the hearer to honest self-examination about their own reception of the word at the specific moment they are hearing it. The private explanation about why Jesus teaches in parables raises the question of insiders and outsiders in terms that have generated sustained theological reflection across every era. The parables that follow press the same affirmation from different angles: the kingdom is underway, its growth is real regardless of appearances, and its final scope will be disproportionate to its present form.

Peter's confession at Caesarea Philippi arrives at the precise narrative midpoint and is the hinge on which the entire Gospel turns. It is the first correct human identification of Jesus in the narrative. But its inadequacy is revealed immediately when Jesus' first explicit passion prediction generates Peter's rebuke — and

Jesus' counter-rebuke. Peter has grasped the title. He has not grasped its content. The Messiah must suffer and be killed and after three days rise again. The *must* is the word that the second half of the Gospel will press from every available angle, because the resistance to it runs deeper than any single statement can dislodge.

The Journey Toward Jerusalem

Chapters 8 through 10 are organized around three cycles, each following the same structure: passion prediction, failure of understanding, teaching about discipleship. The repetition is not redundancy. It is the formal expression of the resistance the teaching is working against, which is deep enough to require the same argument from three different approaches at three different points in the journey. After the first passion prediction, Peter rebukes Jesus and is rebuked in return. After the second, the disciples argue about greatness and are taught that the greatest is the servant of all. After the third, James and John ask for the best seats and are taught that genuine participation in the kingdom means sharing the cup and the baptism of the one whose kingdom it is.

The transfiguration in chapter 9 interrupts the journey to provide the disciples with a glimpse of the glory that is on the other side of the cross they are being prepared for. The divine voice repeats the declaration of the baptism with a specific addition: *listen to him*. The instruction is addressed to disciples who have just demonstrated at Caesarea Philippi that listening has not been their characteristic response to the passion teaching. The transfiguration does not resolve the confusion. It provides the authoritative counter-testimony that the reader can hold against the darkness of what is coming.

Jerusalem and the Passion

The entry into Jerusalem opens the second great confrontation section of the Gospel. Jesus rides into the city on a donkey, greeted by shouts of hosanna from people who are expecting the arrival of the Davidic kingdom in a political form. The week that follows will redefine what the kingdom's arrival actually looks like. The cleansing of the Temple — placed inside the cursing and withering of the fig tree — creates an interpretive frame in which each story illuminates the other. The fig tree with leaves but no fruit interprets the Temple with activity but no genuine prayer. Both are addressed by the one who comes looking for what they were created to produce and finds the substitutes that institutional life generates when the original purpose has been displaced.

The Gethsemane account is among the most intimate passages in Mark. *Father, take this cup from me. Yet not what I will, but what you will.* Jesus prays three times while the disciples sleep three times. The crucifixion is spare and relentless. The darkness at noon is not explained. The cry of dereliction is allowed to stand without softening. And then the centurion's confession: *Surely this man was the Son of God.* The declaration that opens the Gospel in its first verse is confirmed at the climax of the narrative by the last person anyone would have expected, at the last moment anyone would have expected it to come.

The resurrection narrative is compressed and deliberately unsettling. The women come to the tomb. The stone is rolled away. A young man in white tells them that Jesus has risen and instructs them to tell the disciples and Peter that he is going ahead of them to Galilee. And then: *they said nothing to anyone, because they were afraid.* The story does not end. It opens. The reader is left where the women were, with the evidence of resurrection before them and the question of what to do with it still pressing and unanswered — and that, characteristically, is exactly where Mark intends to leave them.

The Meaning of the Whole

Reading Mark's narrative from beginning to end — attending to the way the two-part structure builds toward and through the hinge at Caesarea Philippi, the way the threefold passion prediction cycle presses its argument about discipleship with sustained insistence, the way the intercalations and pairings reveal connections the surface of the narrative does not state, the way the open ending places the reader inside the story rather than outside it — produces an understanding of the whole that is qualitatively different from anything achieved by engaging individual episodes in isolation.

Mark is a carefully constructed argument about the identity of Jesus and the cost of following him, made through narrative rather than through systematic theology. Its claim is that in this specific person, at this specific moment, something has happened that cannot be evaluated by the categories available before it happened — that the Son of God is the crucified one, that the resurrection follows the cross and cannot be separated from it, and that following Jesus means following him in the same direction he moves, which is consistently toward suffering and through it toward life. These claims are not stated once and left at that. They are pressed from every angle across the entire narrative, each episode contributing to the cumulative argument the whole is building.

The story Mark tells is the argument Mark makes, and understanding the argument requires following the story all the way to its deliberately unresolved end. The reader who follows it there will find themselves in the same position as the women at the tomb — with the most significant claim in human history before them and the question of what to do with it still open. That, finally, is the destination toward which the entire narrative has been moving. Not a conclusion that resolves the tension and allows the reader to set the book down satisfied, but a moment of confrontation that opens rather than closes, that presses rather than rests, that places the urgency of the whole Gospel squarely into the hands of the person who has just finished reading it.

The Controversies as Structural Argument

One dimension of Mark's narrative structure that rewards closer attention is the deliberate organization of the controversy stories into patterns that accumulate meaning across the Gospel rather than functioning as independent episodes. The five controversies in chapter 2 and chapter 3 are not random encounters between Jesus and his critics. They are a carefully sequenced escalation: from questioning in the mind to public confrontation to formal accusation to conspiracy to eliminate. The sequence moves with the same purposefulness as the healing accounts that bracket it, and the two kinds of episodes — demonstrations of authority and challenges to that authority — are designed to be read against each other. The healings establish the reality of Jesus' authority; the controversies establish the resistance that authority provokes; and together they move the reader toward the question that organizes the entire first half of the Gospel: who is this person, and what is the source of what he does?

The controversy over Beelzebul in chapter 3, which represents the first climax of the escalating opposition, is particularly important for understanding Mark's narrative logic. When the scribes who have come down from Jerusalem declare that Jesus casts out demons by the prince of demons, they are not simply misidentifying the source of his power. They are demonstrating the logical endpoint of the resistance that the previous controversies have been building toward: the most extreme explanation available within a framework that cannot accommodate the actual explanation. Jesus' counter-argument — that a house divided against itself cannot stand — is not merely clever debate. It reveals what the Beelzebul accusation is actually doing: denying the obvious rather than adjusting the framework that makes the obvious unacceptable. The controversy stories in Mark are, in this sense, as much a portrait of what happens to human frameworks when they encounter something they cannot contain as they are a portrait of the one who generates that encounter.

Chapter 5

Key Themes

*"The time has come. The kingdom of God has come near. Repent
and believe the good news."*
— Mark 1:15

The Kingdom of God

No theme is more central to Mark's Gospel than the kingdom of
God. When Jesus opens his public ministry with the
announcement that the kingdom has come near, he is not offering
a general spiritual framework or an inspiring vision for human
flourishing. He is declaring that what God has been moving
toward throughout Israel's history has now arrived in historically
specific, tangibly demonstrable form — and that the appropriate
response is not reflection but repentance and belief. This
announcement is not the beginning of the story. It is the
declaration that the story has reached its decisive moment and that
nothing can proceed as it did before.

The kingdom in Mark is simultaneously present and urgent.
Its arrival is demonstrated in the exorcisms — the powers that
hold human beings captive are being displaced. In the healings —
the conditions of diminishment characteristic of the old order are
being reversed. In the table fellowship with sinners — the social
boundaries that the old order policed are being dissolved. In the
death and resurrection — the ultimate power of the old order,
death itself, is defeated from within rather than avoided from
without. Every dimension of Jesus' ministry in Mark is a
dimension of the kingdom's arrival, and every response to Jesus
— whether astonishment, faith, hostility, or flight — is a response
to the kingdom he announces and embodies.

The parables of chapter 4 press the kingdom's character from the angle of hiddenness and growth. The kingdom is like seed scattered on the ground that grows while the farmer sleeps — a growth produced by God's action rather than human management and therefore not subject to human anxiety or human acceleration. It is like a mustard seed, smaller than all other seeds, that grows into something large enough for birds to nest in. The kingdom has arrived in hidden form and is moving toward visible completion, and the community that forms around Jesus is the community that lives within this tension — already receiving the kingdom's gifts and already called to embody its values, while the full harvest remains ahead. Mark does not pretend this is comfortable. It is the genuine condition of the community of faith in every era, and the community that takes it seriously will find that the tension between present possession and future completion is generative rather than paralyzing.

The Costliness of the Kingdom

Mark's treatment of what it costs to enter the kingdom is among the most direct and unsoftened in the New Testament. When the rich man comes to Jesus asking what he must do to inherit eternal life, and Jesus tells him to sell everything and give to the poor, the man's face falls and he goes away sorrowful. Mark does not soften the departure or provide the extended reflection that might make it easier to receive. He records the man's exit and then records Jesus' observation: *how hard it is for the rich to enter the kingdom of God.* The statement is not rhetorical. It is a factual observation about what the kingdom requires and what attachment to wealth makes impossible.

The disciples are astonished. If a man who has kept the commandments from his youth cannot enter the kingdom, who can? Jesus' answer — *with man this is impossible, but not with God* — does not make the demand less demanding. It relocates the resource for meeting it. The kingdom's demands are genuinely costly, and their costliness reflects the kingdom's insistence on being the organizing center of a life rather than an addition to a life organized around other centers. Mark's Jesus does not negotiate this requirement or soften it for audiences that might find it difficult. He states it, observes it refused, and uses the refusal as an occasion to teach his disciples about what they have just witnessed and what it means for their own lives.

The Authority of Jesus

The sustained concern with the question of authority runs through the entire Gospel and constitutes one of its central theological arguments. The crowds' astonishment at Capernaum — *he teaches as one having authority, and not as the scribes* — is the first explicit recognition of something that has been implicit in the narrative from its opening verses. The authority the crowds recognize is not primarily rhetorical or intellectual. It is the authority of a presence that operates differently from anything they have encountered within the existing frameworks for religious authority, and the difference is not one of degree but of kind.

The demonstrations of authority that follow in the early chapters establish its scope systematically and cumulatively. Authority over unclean spirits — they obey him. Authority over disease — the fever leaves, the leprosy is cleansed, the paralytic walks. Authority over sin — your sins are forgiven, which generates the controversy that establishes the theological stakes most explicitly. Authority over nature — the wind ceases, the waves flatten, and the disciples ask who this is that even the wind and the sea obey him. Authority over death — Talitha cumi, and the twelve-year-old girl gets up. Each demonstration extends the scope of what has been established in the previous ones, and the cumulative effect is a portrait of authority that has no natural ceiling within the narrative world of the Gospel and that points inevitably toward the identity the Gospel declared in its opening sentence.

Discipleship and the Cost of Following

Mark's Gospel is more searching and less comfortable in its portrait of discipleship than any other account in the New Testament. The three passion prediction cycles in chapters 8 through 10 organize the central teaching on what following Jesus requires around a recurring structure: prediction, misunderstanding, teaching. The structure is precise and deliberate. Each failure of understanding becomes the occasion for a teaching about discipleship that responds to the specific form the failure has taken. Arguing about greatness generates the teaching about being last and servant of all, with the child placed in the midst as the embodied image of what the kingdom's values look like in practice. Requesting positions of honor generates the teaching about the cup and the baptism that genuine sharing in the kingdom requires.

The call to take up the cross in chapter 8 is issued not to an elite of especially committed disciples but to the whole crowd. The demand is universal, and the pattern it describes is the pattern of the one followed: the Son of Man who came not to be served but to serve and to give his life as a ransom for many. Those who follow him exercise the authority they have been given in the same mode — through service rather than domination, through the willingness to give rather than the determination to accumulate, through the movement toward the last place rather than the competition for the first.

The Messianic Secret

One of the most distinctive and most discussed features of Mark's Gospel is the pattern of commands to silence that runs through its first half. Those who are healed are instructed to say nothing. The unclean spirits who recognize Jesus are silenced. The disciples who witness the transfiguration are told to tell no one what they have seen until the Son of Man has risen from the dead. This pattern, which scholars have called the messianic secret, is not a historical strategy of concealment. It is a theological argument about the conditions under which Jesus' identity can be rightly understood.

Demons know who Jesus is but cannot function as witnesses, because their knowledge is accurate but decontextualized — they identify without understanding. The crowds recognize his power but cannot understand its source. Peter confesses his identity but immediately demonstrates that he has grasped the title without grasping its content. True understanding of who Jesus is requires the cross and resurrection, because those events are the fullest expression of what his identity means. This is why the centurion's confession at the foot of the cross is the climactic human identification of Jesus in the Gospel. It comes at the moment when the cross is complete, and the secret is no longer being kept because the conditions for genuine understanding have finally been met.

Suffering and the Son of Man

The title Jesus uses most consistently for himself in Mark is Son of Man, drawn from Daniel's vision of a figure coming on the clouds of heaven with authority and glory. In Mark this title is used in three distinct but related ways that together constitute the Gospel's most sustained Christological argument. The first use establishes present authority on earth — the authority to forgive sins, the authority over the Sabbath. The second use, which dominates the central section and which the disciples most consistently fail to understand, establishes that this authority moves toward suffering: the Son of Man must suffer, be rejected, be killed, and after three days rise again.

The third use is eschatological — the Son of Man coming on the clouds of heaven with power and glory. This future coming stands in deliberate tension with the present suffering, held together by the same title so that neither can be isolated from the other. The one who comes in glory is the one who was crucified. The one who was crucified is the one who comes in glory. Mark uses the Son of Man title to prevent the reader from separating these dimensions into two different figures or two different stories. They are the same person, the same story, and the full portrait requires holding both without resolution into either.

The Temple and True Worship

Mark's engagement with the Temple constitutes one of its most concentrated theological arguments. The cleansing placed inside the fig tree narrative creates an interpretive frame in which each story illuminates the other. The fig tree with leaves but no fruit interprets the Temple with activity but no genuine prayer. Jesus' quotation from Isaiah — *my house shall be called a house of prayer for all nations* — is drawn from a passage about the inclusion of foreigners within the covenant community. The market that has displaced the prayer occupies the court of the Gentiles, the space designated for the nations whose inclusion the prophets had promised. The cleansing is not merely a protest against commercial exploitation. It is a prophetic action that addresses the gap between institutional form and genuine covenant faithfulness, and the prediction of the Temple's destruction in chapter 13 states explicitly what the cleansing and the fig tree have already implied: what fails its purpose irreparably will be removed.

Judgment and Accountability

Mark's Gospel contains some of the most searching passages about divine accountability in the New Testament, concentrated in the eschatological discourse of chapter 13 and in the parabolic material of the final week. The discourse is addressed to four disciples on the Mount of Olives in response to their admiration of the Temple's impressive stonework. Jesus' prediction of the Temple's destruction opens a discourse that ranges from the near future to the distant horizon of the end, maintaining throughout the same concern for faithful endurance under pressure that characterizes the community the Gospel addresses.

The discourse distinguishes carefully between the destruction of the Temple, which is an event within history, and the coming of the Son of Man, which is an event of cosmic finality. False messiahs and wars and earthquakes and persecutions are not the end but the beginning of birth pains — the conditions within which the community must hold fast rather than being misled by premature announcements of the end. The parable of the doorkeeper that concludes the discourse is concentrated to its essential point: a man goes on a journey, leaves his servants in charge, each with their assigned work, and commands the doorkeeper to keep watch. The return is unexpected. The instruction is the same in every case: watch. The community that Mark addresses is not given a timetable. It is given a posture — not anxious calculation about when the end will come, but faithful engagement with the work assigned, combined with the readiness that knows the master may return at any moment.

The Universal Scope of the Gospel

Mark's Gospel moves from its most concentrated focus — a single figure in Galilee, a small group of disciples, a ministry confined to the villages and shorelines of a remote province — to its most expansive horizon: go into all the world and preach the good news to all creation. This movement is not announced at the beginning and developed systematically. It is embedded in the structure of the narrative in ways that prepare the final commission without stating it prematurely.

The seeds of this universality are planted in the earliest chapters. The exorcism in the Capernaum synagogue is witnessed by a crowd that spreads the news throughout the surrounding region. The healing of the leper restores him to the community from which his condition had excluded him. The healing of the Gerasene demoniac takes place in Gentile territory and ends with the restored man being commissioned to tell his own people what Jesus has done — the first mission Jesus authorizes in the Gospel, given to a Gentile in a Gentile region. The feeding of the four thousand takes place on the Gentile side of the sea. The Syrophoenician woman's persistence secures healing for her daughter in a scene that acknowledges the mission's scope extends beyond Israel even before the final commission makes it explicit. The universality of the kingdom is not an afterthought added at the end. It is a thread woven through the entire narrative, surfacing repeatedly in ways that prepare for the final word the risen Jesus sends out into the world.

The Death That Interprets Everything

No theme in Mark is more pervasive or more theologically weighted than the death of Jesus, and no event in the narrative does more interpretive work than the crucifixion. The passion narrative that occupies chapters 14 through 16 is not an appendix to the Gospel. It is the destination toward which the entire narrative has been moving from the moment the Pharisees first conspired with the Herodians about how to destroy Jesus in chapter 3.

The anointing at Bethany in chapter 14 establishes the interpretive frame for the passion that follows. An unnamed woman breaks an alabaster jar of expensive perfume and pours it over Jesus' head. The disciples object to the waste. Jesus defends her: she has done a beautiful thing, and she has anointed his body beforehand for burial. The extravagance that the disciples read as waste, Jesus reads as preparation — and the act of preparation is simultaneously the act of genuine recognition. This woman has understood what is coming with a clarity none of the disciples have demonstrated.

The cry of dereliction from the cross — *My God, my God, why have you forsaken me?* — is the most theologically challenging moment in the Gospel. It is drawn from Psalm 22, a psalm of lament that moves from abandonment to vindication, but Mark does not include the vindication. He allows the cry to stand in its full darkness. The darkness that falls at noon, the silence of the God who has been present throughout the narrative, the mocking of those who misunderstand the cry as a call to Elijah — all of these surround the cry without explaining it away. The explanation is the resurrection, and the resurrection has not yet happened. Mark requires the reader to remain in the darkness before arriving at the light of the empty tomb, because the sequence matters: the darkness is real, the abandonment is genuine, and the resurrection that follows is a resurrection from death rather than a rescue before death arrives.

Chapter 6

Where People Get It Wrong

*"Whoever wants to be my disciple must deny themselves and take
up their cross and follow me."*
— Mark 8:34

Reducing Mark to a Collection of Miracle Stories

The most common misreading of Mark treats its narrative as a
collection of impressive but essentially disconnected miracle
stories — a Gospel best suited for those who want the action
without the extended teaching. On this reading, Mark is the
abbreviated version of the story, the one you read when you want
something vivid and fast-moving rather than theologically
demanding. Each episode is received as a self-contained
demonstration of divine power with its own independent
significance, and the reader moves from one to the next without
attending to the patterns that connect them.

This reading misses everything Mark's structure is doing. The
miracle accounts are not independent demonstrations arranged for
general inspiration. They are arguments — cumulative, sequential,
structurally organized arguments about the nature and source of
Jesus' authority that develop across the narrative and require the
whole to be understood in light of the whole. The exorcism in
Capernaum establishes the scope of that authority. The healing of
the leper extends it to the socially excluded. The healing of the
paralytic connects it to the forgiveness of sins. The stilling of the
storm forces the explicit question — *who is this?* — that all the
previous healings have been pressing toward. Each episode yields

something in isolation. In sequence, they yield an argument that no single episode can carry alone, and the argument is the point.

The practical consequence of reading Mark as a collection of miracle stories is the invisibility of its theological architecture. The two-part structure, the intercalations, the threefold passion prediction cycle — none of these patterns are visible to a reader moving through individual episodes without attending to the connections between them. The Gospel becomes a sourcebook for inspirational narratives rather than the sustained argument about identity and discipleship it was constructed to make. Recovering Mark's structural intentionality is not a specialist's interest. It is the precondition for reading the Gospel as its author designed it to be read and for receiving the argument it was designed to press.

Misunderstanding the Messianic Secret

The messianic secret is among the most consistently misunderstood features of Mark. The commands to silence are frequently read as evidence of a historical strategy — Jesus was managing the pace of his disclosure, avoiding premature political confrontation, or controlling the trajectory of his ministry toward Jerusalem. These explanations all fail before the most obvious evidence: the commands to silence are consistently disobeyed. The healed leper tells everyone. The Gerasene demoniac is explicitly commissioned to tell his own people. The news spreads regardless of instructions to the contrary. If the commands represent a historical strategy, it is one that fails completely and immediately, which would make it one of the least successful strategies in the history of public relations.

As Chapter 5 established, the messianic secret is a theological argument about the conditions for genuine understanding, not a practical strategy of concealment. It is a claim about epistemology — about what kind of knowing the identity of Jesus requires and what events must have occurred before that knowing can become genuine understanding. The silence commands are not practical directives but theological markers: they identify the gap between knowing and understanding that the cross and resurrection must close, and they invite the reader to examine whether their own knowledge of Jesus has crossed that gap or remains on the near side of it.

Treating the Disciples as Simply Incompetent

Mark's sustained portrait of failing disciples has sometimes generated a reading that treats their failure as simple incompetence — a contrast class whose obtuseness serves to highlight Jesus' clarity by contrast. On this reading, the disciples who argue about greatness immediately after a passion prediction, who cannot stay awake in Gethsemane, who flee at the arrest, are simply poor disciples whose example warns us against similar patterns. The lesson is cautionary: don't be like them.

This reading flattens a portrait that is doing considerably more complex theological work. The disciples are not failing because they are unusually slow or spiritually deficient. They are failing because they are confronting something that their available categories genuinely cannot accommodate. The claim that the Messiah must suffer and be killed is not a difficult theological proposition that a sharper mind would have grasped sooner. It is a genuinely unprecedented claim that no available version of messianic expectation had prepared anyone to receive. The disciples' resistance to the passion predictions is not willful stupidity. It is the natural response of people whose theological framework is being asked to include something it was not built to contain and whose inclusion requires not merely more information but a fundamental reorganization of everything they thought they knew.

Understanding the disciples' failure as structural rather than personal changes its role in the narrative entirely. It is not primarily a cautionary tale about poor individual faith but an honest portrait of what happens when genuine encounter with Jesus runs against the genuine limits of the frameworks through which people approach him. The disciples who fail in Mark are the ancestors of every community that has found the cost of faithfulness larger than anticipated, and the risen Jesus who names Peter in the resurrection message is addressing every such community as directly as he addressed the original eleven.

Collapsing Mark into Matthew

A pervasive misreading of Mark results not from within the text but from what is imported into it from other Gospels. Because Matthew and Luke both drew on Mark as a source, readers familiar with those Gospels tend to fill in Mark's gaps — adding the extended temptation dialogue to Mark's compressed two-verse account, supplying the Sermon on the Mount to the compressed teaching sections, reading the birth narratives into Mark's silent opening. The harmonizing impulse is understandable; the impulse to reconcile accounts into a unified picture has deep roots in Christian reading of the Gospels and has produced valuable theological work across centuries.

But harmonizing consistently obscures what is distinctive about each Gospel's presentation. Mark's compressed temptation is doing something specific that Matthew's extended dialogue does not do. Mark's opening without genealogy or birth narrative begins in a different place than Matthew, and the difference is not a deficiency to be corrected by borrowing from the fuller accounts. It is a theological choice about where the story of Jesus begins and what that beginning means for everything that follows. The concentrated opening — only the wilderness, the Jordan, a voice — produces a particular kind of encounter with the story that harmonized reading disperses into the familiarity of the already-known.

Misreading the Passion Predictions

The three passion predictions in chapters 8 through 10 are most frequently misread by separating them from the discipleship teaching that immediately follows each one. Extracted from their structural context, the predictions become statements about what is going to happen to Jesus — prophetic anticipations of the Passion with independent theological significance. This reading captures something real but misses the argument the predictions and the discipleship teaching are making together.

The pattern is precise and deliberate. Jesus predicts his suffering. The disciples respond in a way that reveals their failure to understand. Jesus teaches about discipleship in response to their failure. Reading the passion prediction without the discipleship teaching produces a Christology disconnected from ethics. Reading the discipleship teaching without the passion prediction produces an ethic disconnected from its Christological ground. The argument the two together are making — that the shape of the disciple's life is determined by the shape of the one they follow, and that the cross is therefore not only the event that saves but the pattern that forms — requires the two together to be legible, and separating them produces a reading that is theologically incomplete at the most important point.

Misunderstanding Mark's Treatment of the Law

Mark's engagement with the law has generated misreading in both directions. Some interpreters read the controversy narratives about Sabbath and hand-washing as evidence that Jesus is dismissing the Torah and its traditions as obstacles to genuine spiritual life. Others read the same passages as evidence of a relatively minor dispute about interpretive traditions without broader theological significance. Neither reading captures the actual argument Mark's Jesus is making.

The controversies in Mark about Sabbath and purity are not primarily about which Torah regulations should be observed or which interpretive traditions have got the details right. They are about the interpretive principle that governs how Torah requirements are to be understood and applied — the principle that the human good the commandments were designed to serve must govern how disputes about those commandments are decided. When Jesus declares that the Sabbath was made for man and not man for the Sabbath, he is articulating a hermeneutical principle about the Torah's own intention, not dismissing the Sabbath as irrelevant. When he declares all foods clean, he is drawing out the implications of his earlier teaching about what actually defiles a person in a way that reorients the entire discussion of purity around the interior life rather than exterior contact.

Flattening the Urgency of Mark's Call

A final and pervasive misreading of Mark is the domestication of its urgency — the reading that acknowledges the Gospel's distinctive pace and tone while effectively insulating the reader from the demand that urgency generates. On this reading, Mark is the Gospel of action and immediacy, characteristically vivid and fast-moving, which makes it an engaging read and a useful corrective to approaches to Jesus that are too abstract or overly theological. The urgency is appreciated as a literary quality without being received as a personal demand.

This reading is available to anyone willing to maintain a critical distance from the text — to read about the fishermen dropping their nets without asking whether anything in their own hands is being asked for, to read the passion predictions without applying them to the specific shape of their own discipleship, to read the open ending without receiving the instruction it directs to the disciple and to Peter. Mark does not make this distance comfortable. It was not designed to. The Gospel that begins without preamble, moves without pause, and ends without resolution is structured from beginning to end to resist the reading that takes the measure of its demands without submitting to them.

The urgency that characterizes every page is not a literary style. It is the appropriate texture of a narrative about a presence that arrives without warning, calls without extended explanation, and expects a response before all the conditions for comfortable compliance have been arranged. The domestication of Mark's urgency is arguably the most consequential misreading available because it is the most difficult to identify from the inside — it does not require a false interpretation of any specific passage, only the maintenance of a distance that feels like engagement while actually preventing the text from doing what it was designed to do. Mark's most distinctive feature — the relentless pace, the abrupt transitions, the deliberate refusal to slow down for the reader's comfort — is the formal expression of its resistance to being received on any terms other than its own.

Reading Mark's Ending as Deficient

The abrupt ending of Mark at 16:8 has been treated as a deficiency more consistently than as a deliberate theological choice. The longer ending that appears in many manuscript traditions was added because early readers found the abruptness unsatisfying and supplied the resolution that Mark withholds. The impulse to complete what feels incomplete is understandable, but it domesticates the most theologically significant feature of the Gospel's conclusion and eliminates precisely the feature that makes the ending so demanding.

The open ending is the final and most concentrated expression of what Mark has been doing throughout. The story does not close because it is not designed to close. It is designed to press the question it has been building toward — *what do you do with this?* — directly to the reader and to refuse to answer it on the reader's behalf. The women who fled in silence have been given an instruction. The instruction has not been fulfilled within the narrative. The gap between the instruction and the response is the gap into which the Gospel places every subsequent reader, and the question of what fills that gap is the question the Gospel has been pressing from its first sentence to its last.

Misreading the Tearing of the Temple Curtain

The tearing of the Temple curtain at the moment of Jesus' death is frequently read as a symbol of general accessibility — God is now available to everyone, the barriers have come down, the sacred space has been opened to all. This reading captures something real but misses the specific claim Mark is making by placing the tearing where he does and by using the same vocabulary he used for the tearing of the heavens at the baptism.

The tearing at the baptism opens the story. The Spirit descends, the voice identifies Jesus as the beloved Son, and the mission that will climax at the cross begins. The tearing at the crucifixion closes the story. Jesus dies, the veil is torn, and the centurion confesses what the baptismal voice declared. The structural correspondence between the two tearings is not decorative. It is a deliberate argument: the story that begins with the heavens torn open reaches its completion when the Temple curtain is torn from top to bottom, and the two events together define what the story is about. The tearing at the baptism is the opening of the story. The tearing at the cross is its climax. They frame the entire narrative and interpret each other across the sixteen chapters that separate them.

The Temple curtain that is torn is the inner curtain separating the holy of holies from everything outside it — the space where the presence of God was understood to dwell and into which only the high priest could enter, once a year, on the Day of Atonement. Its tearing is not simply the removal of a barrier in the general sense. It is the end of the system that barrier physically represented — the system of mediated access to God through the Temple's sacrificial apparatus. What is accomplished in the death of Jesus is not the improvement of that system but its completion and supersession. Reading the tearing as a general symbol of accessibility is not wrong, but it is insufficient. It misses the specific argument Mark is making about the relationship between Jesus' death and the Temple system — an argument that has been building through the cleansing, the fig tree, and the prediction of the Temple's destruction, and that reaches its conclusion in the tearing of the curtain at the moment of Jesus' death.

Chapter 7

What It Means for Modern Life

*"Whoever wants to be my disciple must deny themselves and take
up their cross and follow me. For whoever wants to save their life
will lose it, but whoever loses their life for me and for the gospel will
save it."*
— *Mark 8:34–35*

Living Under the Urgency of the Kingdom

The most fundamental practical implication of Mark for modern
readers is the one the Gospel never stops pressing: the time has
come, the kingdom of God has come near, and the response this
requires is not eventual but immediate. Not the response of
religious orientation or general spiritual interest — but the
specific, costly, practically concrete reorientation of a life
organized around a different center of gravity than the one it was
organized around before. Mark does not give the reader time to
consider this demand from a safe distance. It presses the demand
with the same urgency it pressed on the first disciples — not
eventually, not when conditions are favorable, but now, in the
specific circumstances of the specific life one is already living.

Living under the urgency of the kingdom means, practically,
that the standards of discipleship Mark commends in the central
teaching sections of chapters 8 through 10 are not ideals to be
pursued at one's own pace within a life organized around other
primary commitments. They describe the shape of a life genuinely
reoriented toward the one who calls — a reorientation that has
practical consequences for the specific priorities, relationships,
financial choices, professional ambitions, and daily habits of the

person who takes it seriously. The person who takes Mark's call seriously as more than inspiring narrative will find it reorganizing priorities precisely at the points where the surrounding culture — which tends to organize life around the accumulation of security, the exercise of authority over others, and the maintenance of social position — pushes in the opposite direction.

The first and most foundational feature of life shaped by Mark's call is this: it is organized around following rather than leading, around giving rather than accumulating, around willingness to be last rather than determination to be first. This is not a call to passive withdrawal from the world's work. Mark's Jesus is the most active figure in his Gospel — constantly engaging, constantly moving, constantly pressing toward what his mission requires. The call is not to inactivity but to a different kind of activity, organized around a different set of values and moving in a different direction than the activity the surrounding culture commends. When Jesus asks whether it profits a person to gain the whole world and forfeit their life, the question addresses the precise condition of people who are organizing their lives around the goods the surrounding culture promises and finding that the accumulation of those goods does not produce what it promises.

The Practical Reordering of Ambition

The implications of following Mark's Jesus are more specific and more demanding than most discipleship frameworks acknowledge. The dispute about greatness that immediately follows the second passion prediction is not a minor pastoral incident preserved in the narrative for general edification. It is a representative portrait of the human tendency to organize relationships around hierarchy, to measure worth by position, and to treat proximity to power as the primary measure of success in any domain of life. The disciples who have just heard that the Son of Man will be handed over and killed are arguing about which of them is greatest. The juxtaposition is deliberate. Mark is identifying the gap between the pattern of the one they follow and the pattern they are instinctively reproducing, and the gap is not small.

Jesus' response — sitting down, calling the twelve, placing a child in their midst — is a concentrated teaching about what greatness means within the kingdom. *Whoever wants to be first must be last and servant of all.* The child placed in the midst is not a symbol of innocence or spiritual purity. In the social world of first-century Palestine, a child was among those with the least social standing, the least economic utility, and the fewest claims on the attention of people who organized their lives around honor and status. To welcome a child is to welcome the one from whom there is nothing to gain — the one whose welcome costs rather than benefits in the economy of social exchange that governed public life.

For modern readers living in professional environments shaped by the values of competitive achievement and hierarchical advancement, this teaching creates a specific and demanding challenge. It is not a challenge that can be met by performing occasional acts of service while organizing one's professional life according to the logic of advancement and positioning oneself strategically for the next level. It is a challenge to the fundamental orientation of one's ambition — to what success means, to what authority is for, and to what the accumulation of position and influence is supposed to accomplish in a life organized around the kingdom rather than around the goods the surrounding culture offers.

The request of James and John in chapter 10 — for the right to sit at Jesus' right and left in his glory — is not evidence of exceptional arrogance unique to these two disciples. It is the natural expression of an understanding of the kingdom shaped by the wrong categories. They have absorbed the title of Messiah without absorbing what that title means in Mark. They understand the destination but have not understood the path. Jesus' response

— *you do not know what you are asking* — is not a rebuke of their ambition as such but an honest assessment of how badly they have misunderstood the nature of what they are requesting. What they are asking for is defined by the suffering they have not yet agreed to share, and the cup and the baptism that constitute genuine participation in the kingdom's coming are the cup of suffering and the baptism of death, not the positions of honor they are anticipating.

The Cost of Following and Its Contemporary Form

Mark's sustained presentation of the cost of discipleship has more immediate relevance to modern life than most readings acknowledge. The problem is not that modern communities of faith are unaware that following Jesus involves some cost. They generally acknowledge this in principle and often celebrate it in theory. The problem is that the costs most readily acknowledged are the manageable ones — the costs that can be absorbed within a life organized around other primary centers without requiring any fundamental reorganization of that life. The cost Mark most insistently presses is the one that most consistently exceeds what manageable acknowledgment can contain.

When Mark's Jesus calls the whole crowd to take up the cross, *cross* was not a metaphor for the general challenges of committed life. It was a reference to a specific and horrifying form of execution that the Roman imperial system employed to eliminate those who threatened its order. To take up a cross was to carry the instrument of one's own death through the public streets as a demonstration of the empire's ultimate authority. The command was issued in direct connection with the passion prediction that immediately preceded it: the Son of Man must suffer, and following him means going in the same direction. For readers who live in contexts where Christian commitment does not typically involve the threat of execution, the risk of mistaking comfort for faithfulness is real and persistent.

But the cost of following in Mark is not limited to its most extreme expressions. The disciples' call to leave nets and boats and father, the rich man's inability to leave his possessions, the crowds' enthusiasm that evaporates as the demands of the journey toward Jerusalem become clear — these describe the cost of following at every level at which it is experienced, from the most dramatic to the most ordinary. The question Mark presses is not primarily whether one is willing to die for Jesus but whether one is willing to lose whatever one is holding most tightly in response to his call. The answer to that question reveals, in concrete and specific terms, the actual shape of one's discipleship — not its theoretical commitments but its practical realities.

Failure and Restoration as the Normal Pattern

One of Mark's most immediately relevant contributions to modern life is its honest portrayal of the pattern of failure and restoration that characterizes discipleship in every generation. The disciples who flee at the arrest, who fall asleep in Gethsemane, who argue about greatness on the road to Jerusalem are not presented as exceptional failures whose example warns us away from similar patterns. They are presented as the representative disciples of every community that has followed Jesus — people who are genuinely called, genuinely responsive, and genuinely inadequate to the full scope of what the call requires when the conditions for living it out become genuinely demanding.

The resurrection message that specifically includes Peter — *tell the disciples and Peter* — is one of the most pastorally significant moments in the entire Gospel. Peter has just denied Jesus three times, exactly as Jesus predicted he would and exactly as Peter promised he would never do. His inclusion by name in the resurrection message is not an oversight corrected. It is a specific act of targeted, unearned restoration directed at the specific person whose failure was most public and most complete — the one who had insisted most loudly that he would never do what he did. The risen Jesus goes ahead to Galilee — to the place where the whole story began, to the community whose failure was most comprehensively demonstrated in the events of the Passion Week.

For modern communities of faith that know their own patterns of failure — their arguments about greatness, their instinct toward self-preservation, their tendency to fall asleep when watchfulness is most needed — this pattern is among Mark's most sustaining contributions. The community that has failed is not abandoned. It is preceded by the one who goes ahead, who is going ahead still, and who issues the same invitation to follow that was issued beside the Sea of Galilee before the failure happened. The restoration is not earned by subsequent performance. It is given in advance of the performance it makes possible, and it is given specifically, named by name, to the people whose failure was most specifically narrated.

The Widow's Offering and the Economy of the Kingdom

The account of the widow's offering in chapter 12 is among the most compressed and most searching economic teachings in the Gospel. Jesus sits opposite the Temple treasury and watches the crowd putting money in. Many rich people throw in large amounts. A poor widow puts in two small coins — all she had to live on. The contrast the narrative establishes is not primarily financial. It is a contrast between the economics of abundance, where giving costs nothing that cannot be recovered and nothing that one was depending on, and the economics of the kingdom, where giving costs everything and leaves nothing held in reserve.

For modern readers living in economies of material abundance by historical standards, this teaching creates a specific and uncomfortable challenge. The logic of financial stewardship that most contemporary communities of faith practice is broadly organized around giving out of abundance — calculating a percentage of income to give and organizing the remainder according to principles of financial prudence that the surrounding culture broadly endorses. This is not dishonest, but it is not what Mark's widow represents, and it is not what the teaching is pressing toward. The widow does not give a percentage. She gives what she has to live on — the entire economic foundation of her survival.

Mark does not present this as a model that everyone should immediately replicate in every circumstance without discernment. He presents it as the image of what total self-giving looks like when it is not hedged by the calculation that reserves enough for oneself before giving to others. It is the economic expression of the same posture that the call to take up the cross represents in the domain of physical security: the willingness to give up what one is holding rather than determining in advance what one can afford to give up while retaining the rest. The practical application requires more than simply deciding to give more. It requires honest examination of the relationship between one's financial choices and the actual orientation of one's interior life — of what one's money is for, of what level of material security one regards as genuinely necessary, and of what relationship exists between one's surplus and the need present in the communities around one.

The Temple and the Forms of Religion

Mark's engagement with the Temple has direct implications for how modern communities of faith understand the relationship between their institutional forms and the purposes those forms are designed to serve. The cleansing placed inside the fig tree narrative presents a concentrated portrait of institutional failure:

the Temple has become a marketplace rather than a house of prayer for all nations. The institutional form is present and apparently functioning — there is activity, there is commerce, there are people coming and going — but the purpose for which it exists has been displaced by the activity of institutional maintenance and the extraction of economic benefit from religious obligation.

The implications follow directly for every institution that carries a religious purpose. Every institutional form of religious life faces the structural temptation the Temple represents: the tendency of institutional life to generate its own internal purposes, standards of success, and measures of faithfulness that over time displace the external purposes the institution exists to serve. When institutional survival becomes the primary concern, when the maintenance of existing structures consumes the energy that was supposed to be directed outward toward the world the institution exists to serve, when the metrics of institutional health are all internal rather than external, the dynamic Mark describes is operating with full force.

Mark's response is not the abandonment of institutional form. The community of disciples that Mark describes is itself an institution — structured, with recognized leadership and shared commitments and regular practices. The issue is not whether institutions should exist, but what they exist to serve, and whether the practices that sustain the institution are producing the fruit for which it exists or substituting for it in ways that are visible from the outside. The withered fig tree is the image of an institution that has generated impressive external markers while allowing the interior condition that produces genuine fruit to atrophy, and the question every community of faith faces is whether its external markers are the signs of genuine interior vitality or the increasingly elaborate substitutes for it.

Care for the Vulnerable as Kingdom Practice

Mark's consistent portrayal of Jesus moving toward the margins
— toward the leper, the demoniac, the hemorrhaging woman, the
blind beggar, the children who are brought to him and almost
turned away — describes not only what Jesus does but what the
community that follows him is called to do. The care of the
vulnerable is not a secondary concern to be addressed after the
primary work of worship, community building, and institutional
maintenance is complete. It is itself the expression of the
kingdom's character in the present order — the demonstration
that the power Mark describes is consistently oriented toward
restoration rather than accumulation, toward the margins rather
than the center, toward those who cannot reciprocate rather than
those who can.

The healing of the Gerasene demoniac in chapter 5 offers one
of the most socially comprehensive portraits of restoration in the
Gospel. The man has been driven to the margins of the human
social world entirely — living among the tombs, cut off from
household and community, a figure of terror rather than
belonging. Jesus' restoration of this man is not only a healing of
the individual condition. It is the restoration of a person to the
social world from which his condition had entirely excluded him.
The commissioning that follows — *go home to your own people and tell
them how much the Lord has done for you* — is the restoration of a
person to his community, to his family, to the network of
relationships that constitute a human life rather than a mere
biological existence.

Watchfulness in an Uncertain World

Mark's eschatological discourse in chapter 13 has direct relevance
to modern communities of faith navigating genuine uncertainty
about the future. The discourse is not primarily about when the

end will come — Jesus' explicit statement that no one knows the day or the hour removes calendar-setting from the available responses before it can be seriously considered. It is about how to live faithfully in the period of genuine uncertainty between the ascension and the return, which is the period every community of faith since the first century has inhabited.

The four instructions that close the discourse — *be on guard, be alert, keep watch, watch* — are not four different commands with four different objects. They are four expressions of the same fundamental posture: the active, present-focused attentiveness of a community that knows the master may return at any moment and has therefore organized its life around faithful engagement with the work it has been given rather than around speculation about the timing of the return or anxiety about whether the work is going well by visible measures. The doorkeeper who keeps watch is not doing something extraordinary or heroic. They are doing the ordinary work they have been assigned, with the quality of attentiveness that genuine readiness for the master's return requires — present to the work, not distracted by speculation about what is not yet their concern.

For communities living in an era of rapid cultural change and genuine uncertainty about the future shape of Christian life, this posture is both practically necessary and theologically grounded. The temptation to treat the uncertainty of the present as a reason for paralysis, or to invest primary energy in predicting and planning for what the future will require rather than faithfully engaging the present with what has already been given, is precisely what the discourse's repeated command to watch is designed to address. The community that keeps watch is not the community that has solved the problem of institutional uncertainty. It is the community that has remained engaged with the work it has been given, in the specific conditions of the present moment, regardless of its uncertainty about what the next season will bring.

The Cross as the Shape of Christian Life

The most profound and most demanding contribution Mark makes to modern life is also its most central theological claim: that the cross is not an unfortunate event in the story of Jesus that the resurrection eventually corrects, but the fullest expression of who Jesus is and the definitive shape of the life that following him requires. The community that takes this seriously will find that it reorganizes not only the content of its belief but the texture of its daily practice in ways that touch every dimension of what it means to live as a disciple in the contemporary world.

The cross as the shape of Christian life means, practically, that the orientation of one's existence is organized around giving rather than accumulating, around serving rather than being served, around the willingness to lose what one is holding rather than the determination to protect it at every cost. It means that the measure of a community's faithfulness is not its institutional health, social standing, or cultural influence but whether it is moving in the same direction as the one it follows — toward the places of greatest need, toward the people least capable of reciprocating, toward the forms of service that cost something real rather than the forms that can be offered without genuine sacrifice or genuine risk.

The promise that grounds the cross's demand is embedded in the saying that most directly states the demand: *whoever wants to save their life will lose it, and whoever loses their life for me and for the gospel will save it*. The loss is real. The saving is also real. And the community that has organized its life around the pattern of loss and saving that Mark describes will find that the resurrection Mark announces is not only the past event that confirmed Jesus' identity but the present reality that sustains the community's continuing engagement with a world that needs what only the gospel can give. The cross is not the end of the story. It is the shape of the life that leads to the only ending worth having.

Chapter 8

Modern Reflection

"Whoever has ears to hear, let them hear."
— Mark 4:9

Questions for Engagement with Mark's Gospel

The previous chapter examined what Mark makes possible for modern readers — how its specific teachings on ambition, cost, failure, and care for the vulnerable can be applied as practical resources for daily life. This chapter is concerned with a different question: what Mark does to the reader over time. Not the immediate application of a text to a specific situation, but the slower, less visible formation that happens when a person engages with the Gospel seriously and repeatedly across different seasons of life, bringing each season's specific experience to the text and allowing the text to press its specific demands toward that experience.

One of the most pressing questions facing modern culture is whether genuine encounter is possible in a world shaped by mediation, performance, and the management of impression. The longing for something unmanaged — for contact with a reality that cannot be curated or controlled — is everywhere evident, in the appeal of extreme experience, in the persistent dissatisfaction with forms of digital connection that can be crafted and filtered and presented to maximum advantage, in the sense that the interactions most valued in modern life do not fully satisfy the human need for genuine presence. Mark's Gospel does not address this directly, but its portrait of encounter with Jesus speaks to it with searching relevance.

The encounters Mark describes are not managed. They are disruptive. The fishermen who leave their nets do not arrange their affairs first. The leper breaks every protocol governing his condition before receiving any indication that his approach will be welcomed. The hemorrhaging woman reaches through a crowd to touch a garment without permission or announcement, and Jesus feels the power go out from him before she has identified herself. The Gerasene demoniac runs toward Jesus from among the tombs before any invitation has been extended. These are not encounters conducted on the participants' terms. They are encounters that arrive from outside the framework of expectation and demand a response before the framework can be rearranged to accommodate them comfortably.

The Distinctive Character of Mark's Encounter

Mark's Gospel describes encounter with Jesus with unusual physical and emotional specificity, and this specificity is itself instructive for the reader who brings honest attention to it. Jesus sighs deeply. He is moved with compassion. He is indignant. He marvels at unbelief. He looks around with anger. He falls asleep through a storm that is terrifying his disciples. These are not incidental narrative details that reveal a humanizing dimension of an otherwise distant theological figure. They are constitutive of the portrait Mark is painting — a portrait in which the full physicality and emotional reality of Jesus is as much a part of the theological claim as his authority over unclean spirits and his power to raise the dead.

The physicality of Mark's encounter matters for the formation of the reader because it resists the abstraction that theology tends toward when it becomes primarily a conceptual discipline. It is possible to hold a complex and accurate set of beliefs about Jesus while maintaining a relationship with him that is essentially conceptual — a relationship conducted at the level of ideas about Jesus rather than encounter with the specific person the ideas describe. Mark's insistence on the physical and emotional reality of Jesus works against this tendency by making the object of faith irreducibly specific. The one who commands the storm into silence is the one who was sleeping through it. The one who calls his followers to take up the cross is the one who cries out from his own cross in genuine dereliction. The theological claims cannot be separated from the specific person who embodies them, and the specific person is presented with a physicality and emotional reality that resists being reduced to the claims alone.

The Failure of Managed Discipleship

The emergence of programmatic discipleship — the organization of Christian formation around structured programs, curricula, and measurable outcomes — has produced a specific problem that Mark's Gospel addresses with striking directness. The fundamental problem with managed discipleship is that it is conducted at a level of control over the formation process that genuine encounter with Jesus tends to disrupt and that Mark's portrait of discipleship suggests is itself a form of resistance to the kind of formation the Gospel describes.

When discipleship is primarily a program to be completed, the central question becomes whether the participant has successfully acquired the content and demonstrated the competencies the program identifies as evidence of formation. This is a coherent approach to certain aspects of Christian education. But it is not what the discipleship Mark describes looks like, and its systematic application to the whole of formation produces results that diverge from Mark's portrait in ways that accumulate significance over time. The disciples in Mark are not being formed through a program. They are being formed through a relationship conducted in motion — and the formation that happens is not the acquisition of content but the slow, uneven, frequently disrupted work of having one's framework for understanding reality reshaped by continuous encounter with someone whose framework is different in every dimension that matters.

Anxiety and the Storm

Mark chapter 4 contains one of the most direct pastoral engagements with fear and anxiety in the Gospel — the account of Jesus stilling the storm. The disciples are in a boat, a great storm arises, the waves are breaking in, and Jesus is asleep in the stern. They wake him: *Teacher, don't you care if we drown?* He rebukes the wind and waves — *quiet, be still* — and then asks his question: *Why are you so afraid? Do you still have no faith?*

In an era of documented anxiety among populations with more material security than any previous generation in history, this account has acquired particular relevance precisely because the fear it describes is not the fear of people whose material needs are unmet. It is the fear of people in a boat with someone they have watched heal the sick, cast out demons, and pronounce forgiveness — and who are still afraid when the wind rises. The question Jesus asks is not rhetorical in the dismissive sense. It is a genuine inquiry about the relationship between the disciples' fear and the faith they have ostensibly been building through sustained exposure to the person now asleep in the stern. The windstorm is real. The danger is genuine. The question is whether what they know about the one in the boat is available to them in the moment when the wind is high and the waves are breaking in.

The anxiety epidemic of the contemporary moment is broadly a condition in which people experience the ordinary conditions of their lives as sources of existential threat that must be continuously managed and monitored and addressed before they escalate into catastrophe. The management consumes enormous energy and produces, paradoxically, more anxiety rather than less, because the orientation toward threat that managing anxiety requires makes threat more rather than less visible. Mark's response to this condition is not to offer better management techniques or to minimize the reality of genuine threats. It is to press the question Jesus asks in the boat: what has one's sustained encounter with Jesus actually produced in terms of genuine trust in the specific person who is present — not in a principle of divine oversight but in a person of demonstrated character and demonstrated authority who is present in the same boat?

The Beatitudes of Mark

Mark does not contain the Beatitudes of Matthew's Sermon on the Mount, but its narrative is saturated with the same vision of divine favor moving toward the wrong people, arriving in the wrong places, and producing the wrong outcomes by the standards of every available cultural framework. The healed leper who is supposed to maintain silence instead spreads the news everywhere and cannot be stopped. The Gerasene demoniac who is restored is commissioned to tell his own people what has been done for him, and everyone in the Decapolis is amazed. Blind Bartimaeus, told by the crowd to be quiet, shouts more loudly, and Jesus stops and calls him.

The pattern across these accounts is consistent and cumulative: the people least expected to receive attention, least positioned to demand it, and most consistently excluded from the centers of religious and social life are the ones to whom the Gospel's favor consistently moves. For modern readers in a cultural context that tends to concentrate attention, resources, and social capital in the most visible, capable, and connected, this pattern has both diagnostic and formative value. Diagnostically, it identifies the systematic tendency of human community — including religious community — to organize its attention and care around the capable and the visible rather than the vulnerable and the marginalized. Formatively, the pattern Mark describes produces in readers who genuinely encounter it a recurring challenge to examine the actual structure of their community's attention and care.

The Messianic Secret and the Formation of the Reader

The messianic secret functions not only as a Christological argument about the conditions for genuine understanding of Jesus, as Chapter 5 described, but as a formative device for the reader who enters the narrative already knowing what the disciples do not yet know. The sustained dramatic irony it produces — the reader knows from verse one that Jesus is the Son of God, while the human characters spend eight chapters failing to grasp this — places the reader in a position of apparent epistemological advantage that the narrative then consistently calls into question.

The reader who knows from the first verse that Jesus is the Son of God is in a position structurally similar to the scribes who know exactly which prophet predicted that the Messiah would be born in Bethlehem and show no interest in whether the prediction has been fulfilled. Knowing and understanding are not the same thing, and the disciples who have the advantage of direct, sustained, physical encounter with Jesus demonstrate across the entire narrative that proximity does not automatically produce understanding. The reader who has the advantage of the first verse's declaration is in the same danger of mistaking accurate information for genuine understanding — of knowing the title without grasping its content.

The formation that sustained engagement with the messianic secret produces is the gradual recognition that the gap between knowing and understanding is not a first-century problem that modern readers have transcended by virtue of living after the resurrection and having the full canon of Scripture available to them. It is the characteristic gap of every disciple in every generation, and the command at the transfiguration — *listen to him* — is addressed to the reader as directly as to the disciples on the mountain.

Authority and the Formation of Community

Mark's Gospel contains the most direct confrontation with the dominant model of authority in the New Testament, and its implications for the formation of communities of faith extend in every direction across the contemporary cultural landscape. The defining passage in chapter 10 draws a precise contrast between two fundamentally different models of authority. The model of the Gentile rulers — authority exercised over others, lording it over them, making its presence felt through the weight of its standing — is the model that every human institutional structure tends to default toward, because it most efficiently serves the interests of those who hold authority and most clearly communicates to those who do not that the lines of power have been established.

The model Jesus both describes and enacts is one in which authority expresses itself through service, through the willingness to occupy the lowest position rather than the highest, and through the offering of one's own life for the benefit of those over whom authority is theoretically held. This is not a minor adjustment to the Gentile model. It is a fundamental inversion of the logic that the Gentile model embodies, and the inversion is grounded not in a general ethical preference for humility but in the specific action of the Son of Man who came not to be served but to serve and to give his life as a ransom for many.

The Open Ending as Ongoing Formation

The open ending of Mark at 16:8 is the final and most concentrated expression of what the Gospel does to the reader over time. It does not close. It opens — not into comfortable resolution but into the question that the narrative has been building toward from its first sentence and that the empty tomb finally makes unavoidable: what do you do with this?

The women who fled in silence were not failed disciples leaving the story in disgrace. They were the first people in history to be told that Jesus had risen from the dead, and they received that news in a moment of such concentrated strangeness and terror that silence was the only available response in the immediate instant. The instruction they received — *tell the disciples and Peter* — remains unfulfilled within the narrative. The fulfillment is outside the narrative, in the history of those who eventually did tell, who found their way from silence and fear to proclamation, who discovered that the one who had gone ahead to Galilee was genuinely there when they arrived. The formation that extended, repeated, honest engagement with Mark's Gospel produces is the gradual reshaping of the reader's sense of what is urgent, what is real, and what is worth the cost of genuine discipleship. It is not comfortable formation. It is the formation produced by sustained encounter with a presence that does not wait for favorable conditions — that calls from beside the sea, heals in the synagogue, confronts in the Temple, prays in the garden, and rises from the dead with a message that names the one who most needs to hear it. This is what Mark does to the reader over time. It makes the urgency its subject from beginning to end unavoidable — and it makes the one who generates that urgency irreducibly present, immediate, and demanding of a response that the Gospel itself has no power to make on the reader's behalf.

Forgiveness and the Restoration of the Failed

Mark's treatment of failure and restoration across the final section of the Gospel — the flight of the disciples, the denials of Peter,

the specific inclusion of Peter by name in the resurrection message
— constitutes one of the most pastorally significant contributions
the Gospel makes to the life of communities of faith across every
generation. The practical implications of this pattern for how
communities engage their own failures were traced in Chapter 7.
What remains to be considered here is the formative dimension:
how extended engagement with this pattern over time reshapes
the reader's own relationship to failure, recovery, and the grace
that the resurrection makes available.

The specific naming of Peter in the resurrection message
accumulates its fullest pastoral significance not at first reading but
over time, as the reader who has engaged Mark repeatedly comes
to understand how completely the failure it addresses corresponds
to failure in their own experience. Peter has not simply stumbled
in a moment of weakness. He has done exactly what he promised
he would never do, in a sequence of denials that directly mirrors
the three prayers in Gethsemane and the three sleeping episodes
that preceded them. The failure is complete and symmetrical with
the narrative that built toward it. The restoration is equally
complete and specific: the name that singled Peter out as the one
whose failure was most publicly narrated is the name that singles
him out as the one whose restoration is most specifically
addressed.

For communities navigating the specific challenges of a
cultural moment in which the public failures of Christian leaders
and institutions have generated widespread loss of trust, Mark's
pattern of failure and restoration is both a comfort and a
challenge. The comfort is that the Gospel anticipates failure at the
level of those most central to the community's leadership, and that
the resurrection is specifically addressed to that failure rather than
around it. The challenge is that the restoration Mark describes is
not the restoration of institutional credibility through subsequent
performance. It is the restoration of a person by the specific,
named, unearned grace of the one who was failed. Communities

that have experienced leadership failure can receive this pattern as permission to engage honestly with what happened — to name the failure, to receive the restoration, and to find in both the honesty and the restoration the kind of community that genuine discipleship, rather than the performance of discipleship, actually produces.

Chapter 9

Reflection Questions

*"Whoever wants to be my disciple must deny themselves and take
up their cross and follow me."*
— Mark 8:34

Five Lessons from Mark's Gospel

Mark's Gospel is designed not to be received as information but engaged as a living demand. Its urgency is not a stylistic feature that one acknowledges and sets aside after reading. It is the appropriate texture of a narrative about a presence that arrives before the reader is ready, calls before the conditions for comfortable response have been arranged, and ends before the narrative has provided the resolution it keeps promising. The following questions are offered as entry points for the kind of sustained, honest, repeatedly renewed engagement that the Gospel itself commends — not questions with definitive answers but questions that grow more rather than less demanding as the reader grows and as the circumstances of their life change around them.

These questions are designed to be returned to in different seasons of life and at different stages of understanding, with the expectation that what they yield will change as the reader changes. The person who engages them at thirty will find different things pressing than the person who engages them at fifty or at seventy, not because the text has changed but because the life brought to it has deepened and the specific ways the Gospel's urgency presses against that life have become more visible and more demanding. This is part of what it means to say that Mark is designed to be revisited rather than simply completed.

On the Urgency of the Kingdom

Mark's Jesus announces that the kingdom of God has come near and calls for repentance and belief. What difference does it make whether this announcement is received as genuinely urgent versus merely as an inspiring framework for spiritual orientation? Where in your own experience do you most clearly feel — or most consistently resist — the urgency that Mark's opening proclamation generates?

Before the more specific questions about the kingdom's character and demands can be engaged honestly, the foundational question must be faced: do you believe the kingdom of God has actually arrived, with the urgency Mark's Gospel assigns it? Not in principle, not as a general religious conviction that God's purposes are ultimately working toward some good outcome — but specifically, with the immediacy that produces the fishermen's immediate departure from their nets and the tax collector's immediate rise from his booth. The answer to this question determines the framework within which all other questions about the kingdom are asked. If the kingdom has genuinely arrived with genuine urgency, then the call to take up the cross is not an inspiring metaphor but a present demand. If the kingdom has genuinely arrived, then the failure to respond is not a deferral but a refusal. The difference between receiving the kingdom announcement as genuinely urgent and receiving it as an inspiring framework is not primarily a theological distinction. It is a practical difference that shapes the entire character of the life that flows from it.

Consider the parable of the sower in chapter 4 and the specific conditions it describes. Which of the four kinds of soil most honestly describes your own reception of the kingdom at this point in your life? Not which kind you would most like to be, but which most accurately describes the condition of your actual engagement with the kingdom's claims now. Is the word producing fruit in specific, observable ways, or is it being choked by the competing concerns and anxieties of daily life, or is it receiving initial enthusiasm that does not survive genuine testing? The question the parable is asking is not abstract. It is asking about the specific condition of your specific life at the specific moment you are reading it, and an honest answer requires more courage than a general aspiration.

The parable of the growing seed in chapter 4 — in which the farmer scatters seed and the growth happens while he sleeps, through a process he did not produce and cannot accelerate — invites reflection on the relationship between faithfulness and productivity in your own engagement with the kingdom's work. Where are you tempted to treat the kingdom's advance as dependent on your own effort and ingenuity rather than on the growth that God produces through means that exceed your management? The parable is not a counsel of passivity about response. It is a reorientation of the relationship between what you do and what God does — a reorientation that affects the quality of the faithfulness without diminishing its demand.

The parables of the mustard seed and the lamp press the same question from the angle of scale and visibility. The kingdom begins small and hidden. Its present form does not correspond to its final form. Where in your own life and in the life of your community do you find it most difficult to maintain confidence in the kingdom's ultimate scope and completion when its present form is small, hidden, and apparently inconsequential by the standards of visible success? What would it mean to take seriously the claim that what is present now, however small, is genuinely the kingdom of God rather than a preparation for it?

On the Call and Its Cost

The first disciples leave their nets immediately when Jesus calls. What does the immediacy of their response reveal about the character of the call, and what does your own response to the same call reveal about the condition of your discipleship? What are you holding that the call is asking you to leave, and what prevents you from leaving it? These questions deserve more than a general answer. The person who answers "my career" or "my financial security" in the abstract has not yet reached the specific thing the call is asking for. The specific thing is always more particular, more concrete, and more costly than the general category.

The call narratives in chapters 1 and 2 refuse to slow down for psychological explanation, and the refusal is itself a theological claim: the authority of the one who calls is sufficient to produce the response without requiring the preconditions of deliberation and arrangement that human beings typically need before making significant changes. The question the call narratives press is not whether your circumstances are favorable for following but whether the authority of the one who calls is real enough to you to generate the kind of response that the fishermen's immediate departure represents — a response that moves before the conditions for comfortable movement have been fully established.

Consider the rich man in chapter 10 who comes to Jesus asking what he must do to inherit eternal life and who goes away sorrowful because he has great possessions. The sorrow is genuine — he is not indifferent to what he is declining. Where in your own life is there a genuine sorrow that accompanies the recognition of what discipleship is asking for and what you are not yet willing to give? The sorrow is important because it is evidence that the kingdom's claim is genuinely felt even when it is not yet genuinely obeyed. What would it mean to allow the sorrow to become a turning point rather than a turning away — to allow the recognition that the demand is real to produce the movement the sorrow is resisting?

The disciples' argument about greatness in chapter 9 — occurring immediately after the second passion prediction —

invites the most honest kind of self-examination about the actual orientation of your ambition. Not what your stated values are, but what the observable pattern of your choices reveals about what you actually want. Where does the desire for recognition, status, or influence show up in your daily life in ways that directly correspond to the disciples' argument after the passion prediction? The juxtaposition with the passion prediction is the interpretive key: the question is not whether the desire is present but whether you are aware of the gap it represents between the pattern of the one you claim to follow and the pattern you are actually reproducing in your specific daily life.

On the Disciples and Genuine Discipleship

Mark's disciples are people who genuinely follow and consistently fail. Where do you most recognize your own discipleship in their portrait — in their initial responsiveness, in their persistent misunderstanding, or in their final flight? What does the specific form of their failure most consistently reveal about the condition of genuine discipleship under genuine pressure, and what does the correspondence between their failure and your own most honestly show you about the condition of your discipleship now?

The disciples in Mark are not failing because they are unusually obtuse or spiritually deficient relative to disciples in other eras. They are failing because they are confronting something that their available categories genuinely cannot accommodate, and the resistance their failure represents is the resistance that every disciple in every generation mounts against the claim that the cross is the necessary path of genuine messiahship. The form of their failure — arguing about greatness immediately after a passion prediction, asking for seats of honor on the way to Jerusalem, falling asleep in Gethsemane — is the form that the resistance to the cross takes when it is present in people who genuinely believe in Jesus but genuinely have not yet understood what they believe.

Where in your own discipleship is the gap between what you genuinely believe about Jesus and what you are able to sustain in practice most consistent and most revealing? The person who genuinely believes in the kingdom's values and who consistently finds that the pattern of their choices is organized around different values when the cost of the kingdom's values becomes concrete. The person who is committed in principle to the servant model of authority and who consistently defaults to the Gentile model when their own position is threatened. The person who knows what genuine forgiveness requires and who consistently stops short of it when the person to be forgiven is someone whose offense was real and whose accountability has not been adequate. These patterns of consistent shortfall are not evidence that genuine discipleship is absent. They are evidence that genuine discipleship is present but under-formed — that the work of following that Mark's Gospel describes is still in process, as it is for every disciple who is honest about their actual condition.

The specific inclusion of Peter by name in the resurrection message — *tell the disciples and Peter* — invites reflection on the specific, named, unearned character of the restoration it represents. Peter is not restored because his subsequent performance earned it. He is named in the restoration before the performance that the restoration makes possible. Where in your own experience of discipleship have you received a restoration that preceded the performance it eventually produced? What was the specific form of the failure it addressed, and what did receiving the restoration rather than simply working to recover credibility through performance actually require of you in terms of honest acknowledgment and genuine receptivity?

On the Messianic Secret and Genuine Understanding

The messianic secret raises the question of whether knowing and understanding are the same thing. Where in your own engagement with the claims of the Gospel is there the most significant gap between the knowing that explicit information provides and the understanding that genuine encounter produces? The question is not merely about knowing facts about Jesus versus having a personal relationship with him, though it includes that. It is about the specific ways in which accurate theological information can coexist with a practical orientation toward life that has not yet been shaped by what the information, genuinely received, would require.

The demons who recognize Jesus accurately — *you are the Holy One of God* — are silenced precisely because their recognition cannot function as genuine testimony until the cross has been accomplished. Accurate identification does not automatically produce the understanding that Jesus' identity requires. What areas of your theological knowledge about Jesus have remained at the level of accurate identification without producing the understanding that genuine encounter generates — the understanding that is visible not primarily in what one can articulate about Jesus but in how one lives in response to what one claims to believe about him?

Peter's confession at Caesarea Philippi is immediately followed by his refusal of the passion prediction, revealing that his confession has grasped the title without grasping its content. Where in your own confession of Jesus are you most clearly in Peter's position — holding the right title for the wrong kind of Messiah, believing in Jesus while resisting the cross that defines what his messiahship means for the specific shape of your own life? The question the messianic secret is pressing is not whether you know who Jesus is but whether your knowledge of who he is has genuinely engaged the cross as the fullest expression of that identity and as the pattern your own life is being called to reflect.

The transfiguration account in chapter 9 — where the divine voice says *this is my Son, whom I love, listen to him* — addresses the disciples who have just demonstrated their failure to listen at Caesarea Philippi. The instruction to listen is not a rebuke for having been inattentive but a commission for the rest of the journey. What does it mean to genuinely listen to Jesus in the specific areas of your discipleship where the cost of what he is saying is most acutely felt? Listening in those areas is different from listening where the call aligns easily with what one was already inclined to do. The instruction to listen is precisely the instruction to listen where listening is hardest — where the call of the cross runs against the grain of the life one is currently living.

On Suffering and the Cross

Mark's Jesus describes the cross as the path of genuine discipleship for everyone who would follow him, not for a specific group of especially committed disciples who have chosen a particularly demanding form of Christian life. What does taking up the cross mean in the specific circumstances of your specific life — not in the abstract, not as a spiritual metaphor for difficulty in general, but as the concrete, specific, costly reorientation of your actual daily existence around the pattern of the one who came not to be served but to serve?

The saying in chapter 8 — *whoever wants to save their life will lose it, and whoever loses their life for me and for the gospel will save it* — is among the most demanding in the entire Gospel. Engaging it honestly requires identifying specifically what you are most consistently trying to save: what is the life that you are organizing your resources, relationships, and decisions around protecting? The question is not whether protection of legitimate goods is appropriate. It is whether the pattern of your actual choices reveals an orientation toward saving that the saying identifies as the path to losing — an orientation that is investing the primary energy of your life in preserving what the kingdom is asking you to release.

The widow's offering in chapter 12 — giving out of her poverty, not out of her abundance — invites honest examination of the relationship between your financial choices and the actual orientation of your interior life. Not what percentage of your income you give, but what the total pattern of your financial life reveals about what you actually believe about security, abundance, and what you are willing to give up for the kingdom. The widow is not presented as a model to be replicated without discernment in every circumstance regardless of context. She is presented as the image of the total self-giving that characterizes the orientation of a life genuinely organized around the kingdom rather than around the accumulation of what the kingdom asks you to release.

The Gethsemane account invites a specific kind of honest reflection on the experience of genuine wrestling with what God seems to be asking. Have you had experiences of genuine Gethsemane — experiences in which you knew what faithfulness required and found yourself genuinely resistant to it, in which you asked whether the cup could be removed, and in which submission to the will of God was an act of costly trust rather than serene acceptance? What did those experiences reveal about the nature of the genuine obedience that Mark describes — the obedience that is costly because it is real rather than easy because it has been performed without genuine inner cost?

On the Temple and Institutional Life

The cleansing of the Temple — placed inside the fig tree narrative so that each story interprets the other — invites reflection on the relationship between the institutional forms of religious life you participate in and the purposes those forms are designed to serve.

Where in the communities you belong to is there evidence of the dynamic the fig tree represents — external signs of life without the fruit that the external signs are supposed to indicate? Where is there evidence of the dynamic the Temple represents — institutional activity that has become organized around its own maintenance rather than around the purposes it was created to serve?

The question the Temple narrative is asking is not whether institutions should exist but whether the institutions you participate in are producing the fruit for which they exist. What are the specific, external markers of health by which your community measures its own faithfulness, and are those markers genuinely connected to the interior conditions that produce the fruit the community exists to bear? The withered fig tree is the image of impressive external appearance combined with genuine interior failure, and the question every community of faith faces is whether its external markers are the signs of genuine vitality or the increasingly elaborate substitutes for it.

On the Ending and Its Demand

Mark's Gospel ends at 16:8 with the women fleeing in silence because they were afraid. The instruction they were given — *tell the disciples and Peter* — has not been fulfilled within the narrative. What does it mean that the Gospel ends with this gap between the instruction given and the response made? What does the open ending require of the reader that a closed ending would not require?

The gap the ending opens is not a literary puzzle to be solved by identifying historical or psychological explanations for why the women fled. It is a demand addressed to the reader: the instruction has been given, the response has not been made, and the gap is the space into which the Gospel places every subsequent reader. What specific response has the Gospel been pressing toward in your own engagement with it, and what prevents you from making that response now rather than continuing to hold the instruction at the level of information you possess without having fully acted on it?

The most important question Mark's Gospel raises is the same question it has been raising from its first sentence to its last: what do you do with this? Not what do you think about it, not what theological categories you would use to describe it, not what historical reconstruction best accounts for it — but what do you actually do with the claim that the Son of God has come near, has called, has suffered and died and risen, has gone ahead to Galilee, and is waiting for the response that the women in their fear could not make in the moment the empty tomb required it? The Gospel does not make this response for you. It presses the question toward you and holds the space open. What you do with the space is the question Mark has been asking from its first word to its last.

Questions for Continued Engagement

These questions are a beginning rather than an ending. Mark's Gospel is designed to generate more urgency the more carefully it is engaged — not because it is unclear but because it is concentrated, and concentration generates pressure that more diffuse engagement does not reach. The reader who returns to Mark in six months or a year will find that the questions have not been answered and set aside but have deepened and shifted, not because the Gospel has changed but because the reader has, and because new circumstances have made different dimensions of the Gospel's urgency newly immediate and newly demanding.

The most important thing about these questions is not that they be answered but that they be taken seriously with the same quality of engagement the Gospel itself models — the engagement that does not pause between the encounter and the response, that does not defer the demand until conditions are more favorable, that does not manage the question at the level of reflection while protecting the life from the disruption that genuine response would require. The person who asks honestly, who does not settle for the comfort of accurate information without genuine understanding, who continues to bring the questions back to the text and to the community and to the experience of life lived in light of what the text claims, is practicing the kind of engagement that Mark commends. Not the engagement of those who hear and reflect indefinitely, but the engagement of those who hear and follow — imperfectly, inadequately, and with the full range of failure that Mark's disciples display — in the direction the Gospel has been pointing from its first word to its last.

Chapter 10

Five Lessons

"Whoever wants to be my disciple must deny themselves and take
up their cross and follow me."
— Mark 8:34

Five Lessons from Mark's Gospel

The capacity of Mark's Gospel to shape communities of faith has
not diminished across nearly two thousand years of engagement.
The urgency that characterizes every page of the narrative is not a
feature of the first-century moment that subsequent centuries
have left behind. It is a permanent feature of the kingdom's
presence that every generation must engage on its own terms, in
its own circumstances, with its own specific forms of resistance
and its own specific needs for the restoration that the resurrection
provides. The five lessons that follow are not five separate topics
but five dimensions of a single underlying reality — five angles
from which Mark approaches the central claim that the Son of
God has come near, that following him costs everything and
produces everything, and that the urgency of that claim does not
diminish with familiarity or with the passage of time.

These five lessons are not a summary of Mark's content.
They are a distillation of the most persistent and most demanding
things the Gospel asks of those who receive it — the things that
remain pressing after all the historical context has been provided,
all the structural features have been explained, all the theological
categories have been identified. They are the lessons that remain
when the reader has finished absorbing the information the
Gospel provides and is left with the question the information has
been building toward: what do you do with this? Each lesson is an

answer to that question from a different angle, and together they constitute the response that Mark has been pressing its readers toward from its opening announcement to its open ending.

Lesson One: The Kingdom Demands Immediate Response

Mark's Gospel begins with an announcement and a command: the time has come, the kingdom of God has come near, repent and believe the good news. The announcement is not an invitation to theological reflection or an occasion for the arrangement of one's affairs before responding. It is a declaration that something decisive has happened and that the window for response is open now — not eventually, not when the conditions for response have become more favorable, but now, in the specific circumstances of the specific life one is already living. Everything which follows in the narrative is shaped by this foundational urgency: something has arrived, something unprecedented is underway, and the appropriate response is not deliberation but the total reorientation of the whole self toward the one who has arrived and toward the kingdom his arrival has inaugurated.

The urgency of this announcement is maintained throughout the Gospel with a concentration that is unlike anything in the other Gospels. The word *immediately* — appearing more frequently in Mark than in all the other Gospels combined — is not a stylistic habit or a feature of oral storytelling technique. It is a sustained theological claim about the character of the kingdom's presence and the nature of the response it generates. When Jesus calls, the fishermen leave immediately. When he commands the unclean spirit, it leaves immediately. When he touches the leper, the leprosy leaves immediately. When he says to Jairus's daughter *Talitha cumi*, she gets up immediately. The compressed narrative does not provide the intervals for deliberation and arrangement that human beings typically need before making significant changes because the kingdom's arrival does not accommodate itself to those intervals or wait for them to be completed.

The call to immediate response in Mark is not a call to a particular set of behaviors, though it has behavioral implications that are extensive and specific. It is a call to a particular orientation of the self — to the genuine, total, practically specific reorientation of one's life around the one who calls rather than around the goods the surrounding world offers and the familiar frameworks that organize daily existence into its current patterns. This is why the call narratives communicate the disciples' response through the single word *immediately* rather than through any description of the internal process that produced it. The point is not their psychology but the authority of the one who calls and the adequacy of that authority to produce a response that no other authority available to them could have produced.

The parables of chapter 4 press the call to immediate response from a different and more searching angle. The parable of the sower is not primarily a map of why some people respond to the kingdom and others do not. It is an invitation to the honest self-examination that genuine response requires — to ask not in the abstract but specifically and concretely which of the four conditions described most accurately corresponds to the current condition of one's own reception of the word. The parable of the growing seed insists that the kingdom's growth is not produced by human effort and cannot be accelerated by human anxiety, but this is not a counsel of passivity about the initial response. It is a reorientation of the relationship between faithfulness and productivity — a recognition that what the farmer is responsible for is the faithfulness of the sowing and the watchfulness of the harvest, not the growth that happens in between and that belongs to God rather than to human management.

The specific form that the call to immediate response takes in the contemporary moment is not the same as the form it took in first-century Galilee — most readers of Mark are not being called to leave fishing boats on a specific lakeshore on a specific morning. But the authority of the call is identical, and the tendency to convert its immediacy into the deferred intention to respond when conditions become more favorable is the same tendency that the Gospel's relentless momentum is designed to disrupt in every generation that encounters it. The person who knows what the call is asking and has not yet made the response it requires is not in a waiting period before the response becomes necessary. They are already in the position of the disciples after the first passion prediction — knowing what faithfulness requires and choosing, at least for the moment, the response that Peter's rebuke represents rather than the response that taking up the cross demands. The question is not whether the call has been heard. It is whether it has been answered, and when.

Lesson Two: Genuine Authority Moves Toward the Margin

One of Mark's most consistent and most theologically searching lessons is that the authority Jesus exercises — the authority that the crowds recognize as different in kind from anything the scribal tradition provides — is characterized not by its reach over those below it but by its consistent directional movement toward those at the margins. Every demonstration of Jesus' authority in the first half of the Gospel is a demonstration of authority exercised in the same direction: toward the leper, the demoniac, the hemorrhaging woman, the dead child, the blind beggar, the Gentile woman's daughter. The authority moves toward suffering rather than away from it, toward the excluded rather than toward the already included, toward the restoration of what has been taken rather than the accumulation of what can be gained by those who are already in a position to gain.

This directional consistency is not incidental to Mark's portrait of Jesus. It is the content of the claim that his authority is different in kind from the authority of the scribes and all the other authority figures who populate the Gospel's narrative world. The scribes' authority is centered — it operates from the institutional center outward, adjudicating the conditions under which people may approach the center and maintain their position within it, exercised primarily in the service of those who already have standing rather than those who have been excluded from it. The authority Mark's Jesus exercises is decentered — it moves from wherever Jesus is toward wherever the need is most acute, without reference to the conditions that normally govern who may approach and under what terms, without regard for the social costs of crossing the boundaries that separate the center from the margins.

For modern readers, this lesson has both diagnostic and formative value that extends into every domain of institutional and communal life. Diagnostically, it identifies the systematic tendency of human institutions — including and especially religious institutions — to organize their authority around the maintenance of their own centers rather than the consistent movement toward their margins. The institution whose primary concern is the protection of its existing members, the maintenance of its established practices, the management of its boundaries, and the preservation of its internal culture is exercising authority in the scribal mode rather than the mode that Mark's Jesus both describes and enacts. The fact that the institution carries the name of the one whose authority moved consistently toward the margin does not automatically produce the same directional movement in the institution's own exercise of authority. That movement must be actively chosen, actively practiced, and actively resisted against the structural tendencies of institutional life that consistently pull in the opposite direction.

Formatively, the directional consistency of Mark's portrait produces in readers who genuinely engage it a persistent reorientation of attention toward the margins of the communities they inhabit. The community formed by sustained engagement with Mark's demonstration of authority is the community that has learned — slowly, incompletely, against the structural tendencies of institutional life — to ask where the margins are in its specific context, who is there, what conditions have placed them there, and what movement toward rather than away from those margins would actually look like in the specific circumstances of its specific common life. This is not a question with a single universal answer, because the margins are different in different contexts and the movement toward them takes different forms in different circumstances. But the question itself — pressed repeatedly and honestly by sustained engagement with Mark's portrait of authority — is the question that keeps the community's exercise of authority honest and prevents the drift toward the Gentile model from becoming permanent.

The authority of Jesus that Mark describes is not simply the authority to heal and cast out demons. It is the authority of the Son of God, exercised in the service of the mission for which the Son of God came — to give his life as a ransom for many. Every healing, every exorcism, every crossing of the boundary that separates the center from the margin is an enactment of the same mission that reaches its completion at the cross. The authority that moves toward the leper in chapter 1 is moving toward the cross in chapter 15, and the cross is the final and most complete expression of the same directional movement: toward the greatest need, at the greatest cost, with the greatest result. The community that genuinely learns from Mark's portrait of authority will find that it is being formed not only in the direction of its service but in the willingness to pay the cost that moving consistently in that direction requires — and that cost, Mark is honest enough to say, is not always manageable.

Lesson Three: The Cross Is the Shape of Genuine Life

Mark's third and most demanding lesson is the one that runs through the entire second half of the Gospel with a persistence that the three passion prediction cycles make impossible to avoid or to receive only theoretically: the cross is not an unfortunate circumstance of Jesus' particular historical situation that the resurrection eventually corrects, but the definitive shape of the life that genuine participation in the kingdom requires. This is the lesson that the disciples most consistently resist and the one that the Gospel most consistently presses, using different approaches at different moments because the resistance is deep enough to require the same argument from multiple angles before it can begin to penetrate.

The saying in chapter 8 that most directly states this lesson — *whoever wants to save their life will lose it, and whoever loses their life for me and for the gospel will save it* — is addressed not to the disciples alone but to the whole crowd that has gathered around Jesus. The call to take up the cross is not an elite demand made of especially committed disciples who have chosen a particularly demanding form of Christian life. It is the basic description of what following Jesus requires of anyone who does it, regardless of their level of commitment as they understand it, regardless of the specific form their discipleship takes, regardless of the cultural context in which they are trying to live it out. The universality of the demand is itself significant: there is no version of genuine discipleship in Mark that involves following Jesus without the cross, no arrangement of one's discipleship that gets the destination without the path that leads to it, no form of Christian life that can be organized around the resurrection while avoiding the cross that precedes and defines it.

The three passion prediction cycles that organize chapters 8 through 10 develop this lesson from three different angles, each pressing the same claim in response to a different form of the disciples' resistance, and each generating a different specific teaching about what the cross means for the practical shape of discipleship. The first cycle addresses the disciples' resistance to the suffering of the Messiah itself — the claim that the cross is incompatible with genuine messiahship, that a God who wins cannot be a God who suffers — and Jesus' response identifies this resistance not merely as a theological error but as the satanic alternative to the cross, as the temptation to organize one's understanding of God and his purposes around the avoidance of cost rather than its embrace. The second cycle addresses the disciples' resistance to the implications of the cross for their own status and relationship to one another, and Jesus' response defines greatness within the kingdom as servanthood — not as a compensatory spiritual reward for those who have accepted diminished status but as the actual content of what greatness means in a kingdom organized around the pattern of the one who came to serve. The third cycle addresses the disciples' resistance to the specific costs of the cross in their own experience and generates Jesus' most explicit statement of the connection between Christology and discipleship: the Son of Man did not come to be served but to serve and to give his life as a ransom for many, and this is the pattern that defines what it means to exercise authority within the kingdom he inaugurates.

The practical implications of this lesson for contemporary communities of faith are extensive and consistently demanding, and they cannot be reduced to a set of specific practices that one can adopt while leaving the fundamental orientation of one's life unchanged. The community that has organized its life primarily around comfort, institutional health, social acceptance, and the avoidance of the specific costs that genuine faithfulness in the present cultural moment requires has not yet allowed the cross to be the shape of its common life, whatever it may say about the centrality of the cross in its theology. The community that has allowed the cross to be that shape will look genuinely different from the communities organized around self-preservation and institutional maintenance: it will move toward costs rather than away from them, toward the people who cannot reciprocate rather than toward the people who can, toward the forms of service that require genuine sacrifice rather than the forms that can be offered without real loss. It will measure its faithfulness not by the results that are visible and countable but by the quality of its movement in the direction that the cross defines — and it will find that this movement, consistently maintained over time, produces exactly the kinds of fruit that Mark describes and exactly the kinds of cost that Mark prepares its readers for.

Lesson Four: Failure Is Not the End of the Story

Mark's fourth lesson is among the most pastorally significant contributions the Gospel makes to communities of faith in every generation: the pattern of failure and restoration that the disciples display across the final section of the narrative is not an exceptional event in the career of exceptional disciples but the representative pattern of genuine discipleship encountering genuine cost, and the resurrection that addresses that failure is specifically addressed to it rather than around it, specifically named rather than generally promised, given before the performance that would seem to justify it rather than after.

The disciples' failure in Mark is comprehensive in a way that the other Gospels do not quite replicate. They misunderstand Jesus repeatedly and persistently across the entire journey to Jerusalem. They fall asleep in Gethsemane when he has specifically and explicitly asked them to keep watch. They scatter at the arrest, leaving Jesus alone to face what is coming. Peter denies Jesus three times in the courtyard of the high priest in the precise sequence and setting that the narrative has been preparing from the moment Peter made his bold declaration of willingness to die — the symmetry between the promise and the failure is exact, and Mark does not soften it. The failure is not incidental or partial or the product of a momentary lapse under extreme pressure. It is total and it is public and it is visible to everyone who witnessed it, including the servant girl who identified Peter by the fire.

If the Gospel had ended with the crucifixion, the disciples' story would be the story of people who received an extraordinary call, made an extraordinary initial response, participated in an extraordinary ministry, and then failed comprehensively when the call's full cost became clear and unavoidable. The failure would be the last word about them, and the community that formed around their testimony would have to reckon with a founding narrative of abandonment and denial. But the resurrection message does not end with the failure. It specifically addresses the failure by specifically including the person whose failure was most public and most complete: *tell the disciples and Peter.* The risen Jesus does not go to Jerusalem to receive the community that has gathered itself in remorse and penitence. He goes ahead to Galilee — to the place where the story began, to the specific landscape of the initial call, to the precise context in which the community that the Passion dispersed can be reconstituted by the one who has gone ahead to meet them there regardless of what happened between the Sea of Galilee and the courtyard of the high priest.

For communities of faith in every generation that know their own patterns of failure, this pattern is among Mark's most sustaining contributions to the life of the church across time. The comfort is genuine and it must be received as genuine rather than immediately qualified into practical meaninglessness: Mark's Gospel anticipates failure at the level of those most central to the community's life and mission, and the resurrection is specifically addressed to that failure rather than pretending it did not happen or conditioning the restoration on subsequent performance. The demand is equally genuine and must be received with equal seriousness: the restoration Mark describes requires the community to receive it honestly rather than performing a recovery that bypasses honest engagement with what actually happened. The community that can say plainly that it failed — that it fell asleep, that it denied, that it fled — and that can receive the restoration the resurrection offers rather than managing its way back to credibility through institutional performance, is the community most capable of the sustained discipleship that Mark's Gospel actually describes. The pattern of failure and restoration is not a deviation from genuine discipleship. It is, in Mark's honest portrait, its characteristic form in every generation.

Lesson Five: The Resurrection Generates Ongoing Urgency

Mark's fifth and final lesson is the one its open ending embeds most deliberately in the reader who follows the Gospel to its last word: the resurrection does not resolve the urgency the Gospel has been generating from its first sentence but intensifies it, because the risen Jesus who has gone ahead to Galilee is going ahead still, and the instruction given at the empty tomb has not yet been fully obeyed by any generation of disciples that has received it. The urgency that opens the Gospel with the announcement that the time has come and the kingdom of God has come near is not discharged by the resurrection. It is concentrated there, focused to its sharpest point, and directed toward the reader with the full weight of everything the narrative has established about who is making the demand and why the demand is worth everything it costs.

The open ending at 16:8 is not a narrative deficiency or an accident of transmission or an incomplete text waiting for its proper conclusion. It is the deliberate final expression of the Gospel's most fundamental theological claim about the relationship between the resurrection and the community that the resurrection reconstitutes. The women flee in silence because they were afraid, and the instruction they were given — *tell the disciples and Peter* — remains unfulfilled within the narrative. The gap between the instruction and the response is the gap into which the Gospel places every subsequent reader, not as a literary device to be appreciated from a distance but as a demand to be engaged with the same quality of response that the fishermen's immediate departure represented at the beginning of the story. The ending is open not because the story is unfinished but because the story continues in the response of every reader who has followed it to this point and is now left with the question the women faced at the tomb: what do you do with this?

The risen Jesus who has gone ahead to Galilee is not a historical figure whose activity was concluded by the resurrection and whose ongoing presence is now available only in memory, text, and theological reflection. He is the risen Lord who is present and active in the world he has claimed — who goes ahead rather than waiting, who precedes the community's gathering rather than following it, who is already in the place of new beginning before the community that failed has found its way back from the place of failure. This ongoing activity of the risen Jesus is the foundation on which the community's own ongoing activity rests, because the community's mission is not the initiation of a work that would not otherwise exist but the participation in a work that the risen Jesus is already doing in the world he has claimed.

The urgency that the resurrection generates is not the urgency of anxiety about whether the mission will succeed or whether the community is doing enough. It is the urgency of genuine commission — of having been given a specific instruction by a specific person who has demonstrated, across sixteen chapters of relentless movement toward suffering and through it toward resurrection, that his authority is real and his promises are reliable and his restoration of those who fail is as specific and as named as his original call to those who follow. The community that has genuinely received this commission does not need to generate its own enthusiasm as the primary energy of its engagement with the world. It needs only to follow — to go in the direction the risen Jesus has already gone, to participate in the work he is already doing, to tell what has been seen and heard with the urgency that the Gospel has maintained from its first sentence to its last.

The promise that grounds the commission is embedded in the structure of the resurrection message itself: *Jesus is going ahead of you to Galilee. There you will see him, just as he told you.* The one who has been the subject of the Gospel's entire narrative — who called from beside the sea, healed in the synagogue, confronted in the Temple, prayed in the garden, died on the cross, and rose from the tomb — is going ahead. The community that follows will find him there. This is not a vague promise of general divine accompaniment available to those who maintain sufficient faith. It is the specific promise of the specific person whose story Mark has told, made in the specific context of the community's specific failure and the resurrection that addresses it. The promise is as reliable as every other promise in the narrative has proven reliable, and the community that follows the risen Jesus toward Galilee will find, as every generation before it has found, that the one who went ahead was already there.

Mark's Gospel will keep pressing what it has always pressed as its readers keep bringing more to it. The five lessons offered here are five angles on the single reality that the Gospel has been demonstrating from beginning to end: that the Son of God has come near, that following him costs everything and produces everything, that failure is addressed rather than final, and that the risen Jesus who goes ahead to Galilee is going ahead still — into every context where the Gospel is genuinely received, every community where the cross is genuinely taken up, every season of failure where the specific, named, unearned restoration is genuinely needed. The invitation the empty tomb extends is the same invitation the Sea of Galilee extended in chapter one. The authority behind it is the same authority. The response it requires is the same response. And the life that genuine response produces is, as Mark has been insisting from its first word to its last, the only life worth the name.

What Mark Has Given to the World

The influence of Mark's Gospel on the history of communities of faith is both undeniable and frequently underestimated, in part because Mark has so often been read through the lens of Matthew and Luke — as the abbreviated version of a story better told elsewhere, the rough draft that the other Evangelists refined into something more complete. Reading Mark on its own terms, as a sustained and deliberate theological argument rather than as a source for the other Gospels, reveals a depth and a specificity that the harmonizing tradition has consistently obscured.

The conviction that genuine authority is exercised through service rather than domination owes as much to Mark's portrait of the Son of Man who came not to be served but to serve as to any other formulation in the New Testament. The conviction that the cross is not an unfortunate event that interrupts a story of triumph but the central event that defines what triumph means owes its most concentrated narrative expression to the structure of Mark, which moves from the opening declaration of the Son of God to the centurion's confession at the foot of the cross with a deliberateness that makes the connection between identity and suffering impossible to miss for any reader who follows the whole. The conviction that failure does not end the story of discipleship — that the community formed around Jesus can be reconstituted after its most complete failure by the specific, named, unearned grace of the resurrection — is embedded in the structure of Mark's ending in a way that no other Gospel quite replicates.

This does not mean that communities formed under Mark's influence have been consistently faithful to its vision. Institutions that invoke the authority of the Son of God have exercised that authority in the Gentile mode rather than the servant mode. Communities that claim to follow the one who moved consistently toward the margins have organized themselves around their centers. Those who preach the cross have sought the positions of honor that the cross's logic consistently displaces. Acknowledging this history is not a reason to abandon Mark. It is a reason to read it more carefully and more honestly — to allow the text to exercise the same confrontational authority over the communities that read it that it exercised over the Pharisees and scribes and crowds of Galilee and Jerusalem. The portrait of authority Mark presents is not less demanding of the communities that carry it than it was of those who first encountered it in the villages of first-century Palestine.

The Enduring Questions

The questions that Mark's Gospel raises cannot be finally answered by any human arrangement and will therefore continue to press themselves on every community and every individual in every era. They are questions about where genuine authority comes from and what its exercise looks like when it is not corrupted by the logic of domination. They are questions about what the cross means for the specific shape of a community's common life — not as a theological symbol to be displayed but as a practical pattern to be embodied in the specific choices of specific people in specific circumstances. They are questions about what to do with failure — one's own failure, the community's failure, the failure of those one has trusted — and whether the resurrection addresses that failure in the specific, named, concrete way that the message to the disciples and Peter suggests.

These questions are currently being asked with unusual urgency in Western culture, because the institutions that previously provided frameworks for authority, community, and the management of failure have eroded significantly and have in many cases been discredited by the specific failures that their exercise of authority produced. Mark's response to this condition is the same response it has always offered: here is the one whose authority is different in kind from anything the available frameworks have provided; come and see, come and follow, come and discover what the life organized around his pattern actually produces in the specific circumstances of the specific life you are already living.

The Character of Sustained Reading

Reading Mark well over a lifetime requires the cultivation of specific habits of reading that do not develop without intention and practice and repeated return to the text across different seasons of life. The most important is the habit of bringing one's actual experience to the text rather than leaving it at the door. Mark is not designed to be read as a historical account whose significance is independent of the specific circumstances of the reader's life. It is designed to address those circumstances — to engage the actual urgency, actual failure, actual fear, actual longing for genuine authority, and actual need for restoration that constitute the reader's experience at any given moment of encounter. The text meets the reader where they actually are, and the depth of the meeting is proportional to the honesty with which the reader brings their actual situation.

The reader who engages Mark over years and decades will find that sustained engagement produces a specific kind of formation that cannot be achieved in any other way — not the formation of comprehensive theological understanding, but the formation of a person who has been shaped over time by sustained encounter with the specific person Mark describes. Mark's formation of its readers follows the same pattern as the formation of the disciples: it does not require extraordinary preparation or exceptional capacity. It requires the willingness to keep showing up, to keep bringing one's actual experience honestly, to keep allowing the text to press its urgency toward the specific conditions of one's specific life rather than managing the encounter at a comfortable distance.

Closing Reflection

"He has risen! He is not here. See the place where they laid him."
— Mark 16:6

Mark's Gospel has endured because the urgency it carries does not age. *Who is this man, that even the wind and the sea obey him?* What does genuine discipleship look like when the one being followed goes to the cross? What kind of community does the kingdom of God call into being, and by what pattern of failure and restoration is that community sustained across the centuries and the cultures and the specific pressures of each generation's particular moment? These are not questions that belong to the first century alone. They are questions that each generation must face with the honesty and the urgency they deserve, and Mark is designed to make that honest engagement both possible and unavoidable for those who bring sufficient attention to it.

What gives Mark its lasting power is not the vividness of its narrative alone, though that narrative has shaped the imagination of communities of faith more immediately and more physically than any other account of Jesus' ministry. It is the claim at its center — that in the person of Jesus of Nazareth, the Son of God entered the world with the authority to displace every power that diminishes and destroys human life, that he accomplished this displacement through the cross rather than around it, and that the empty tomb is the confirmation that his authority is precisely what the Gospel claimed it was from its opening sentence to its last unresolved word. This claim is either true, or it is not, and Mark does not allow its readers to hold it at a comfortable distance where it can be appreciated without being engaged. It presses toward response with the same immediacy it assigns to every encounter the narrative describes, from the fishermen who left their nets to the women who fled in silence.

One of the most characteristic features of Mark's Gospel, observed across the entire history of its reception by communities of faith in every era and every cultural context, is its resistance to being received passively. Those who bring to it the honest engagement it deserves consistently find that it presses them further than they intended to go, confronts them at levels they did not anticipate, and makes claims on their lives that are more immediate and more demanding than any initial reading could prepare them for. Mark is designed to be revisited rather than simply completed, returned to rather than finished, engaged repeatedly rather than mastered once. Its depth is not all visible on the surface, and its urgency does not diminish with familiarity. The reader who has read it ten times begins to notice the intercalations that require one story to be read inside another, the pairing of episodes that accumulates significance through comparison, the way the open ending illuminates everything that preceded it as a preparation for the response it refuses to provide on the reader's behalf.

What Mark Has Given to the World

The influence of Mark's Gospel on the history of communities of faith is both undeniable and frequently underestimated, in part because Mark has so often been read through the lens of Matthew and Luke — as the abbreviated version of a story better told elsewhere, the rough draft that the other Evangelists refined and completed. Reading Mark on its own terms, as a sustained and deliberate theological argument rather than as a source for the other Gospels, reveals a depth and a specificity that the harmonizing tradition has consistently obscured and that becomes visible only when the text is allowed to say what it says rather than being supplemented with what the other accounts provide.

The conviction that genuine authority is exercised through service rather than domination owes as much to Mark's portrait of the Son of Man who came not to be served but to serve as to any other formulation in the New Testament. The conviction that the cross is not an unfortunate event that interrupts a story of triumph but the central event that defines what triumph means owes its most concentrated narrative expression to the structure of Mark, which moves from the opening declaration of the Son of God to the centurion's confession at the foot of the cross with a deliberateness that makes the connection between identity and suffering impossible to miss. The conviction that failure does not end the story of discipleship — that the community formed around Jesus can be reconstituted after its most complete failure by the specific, named, unearned grace of the resurrection — is embedded in the structure of Mark's ending in a way that no other Gospel quite replicates and that has sustained communities of faith through centuries of their own failures.

This does not mean that communities formed under Mark's influence have been consistently faithful to its vision. Institutions that invoke the authority of the Son of God have exercised that authority in the Gentile mode rather than the servant mode. Communities that claim to follow the one who moved consistently toward the margins have organized themselves around their centers. Those who preach the cross have sought the positions of honor that the cross's logic consistently displaces. Acknowledging this history is not a reason to abandon Mark or to lose confidence in its continuing power to form communities of genuine discipleship. It is a reason to read it more carefully and more honestly — to allow the text to exercise the same confrontational authority over the communities that read it that it exercised over the Pharisees and scribes and crowds of Galilee and Jerusalem. The portrait of authority Mark presents is no less demanding of the communities that carry it than it was of those who first encountered it in the villages of first-century Palestine.

The Enduring Questions

The questions that Mark's Gospel raises cannot be finally answered by any human arrangement and will therefore continue to press themselves on every community and every individual in every era of the church's life in the world. They are questions about where genuine authority comes from and what its exercise looks like when it is not corrupted by the logic of domination that Mark identifies as the Gentile model. They are questions about what the cross means for the specific shape of a community's common life — not as a theological symbol to be displayed but as a practical pattern to be embodied in the specific choices of specific people living in specific circumstances. They are questions about what to do with failure — one's own failure, the community's failure, the failure of those one has trusted — and whether the resurrection addresses that failure in the specific, named, concrete way that the message to the disciples and Peter suggests it does.

These questions are currently being asked with unusual urgency in Western culture, because the institutions that previously provided frameworks for authority, community, and the management of failure have eroded significantly and have, in many cases, been discredited by the specific failures that their exercise of authority produced. Mark's response to this condition is the same response it has always offered: here is the one whose authority is different in kind from anything the available frameworks have provided; come and see, come and follow, come and discover what the life organized around his pattern actually produces in the specific circumstances of the specific life you are already living. The invitation is the same in every era. The authority behind it is unchanged. The life it produces is the life Mark has been describing from its first word to its last.

The Character of Sustained Reading

Reading Mark well over a lifetime requires the cultivation of specific habits of reading that do not develop without intention and practice and repeated return to the text across different seasons of life. The most important is the habit of bringing one's actual experience to the text rather than leaving it at the door in favor of a more polished or more presentable version of one's life. Mark is not designed to be read as a historical account whose significance is independent of the specific circumstances of the reader's life. It is designed to address those circumstances — to engage the actual urgency, actual failure, actual fear, actual longing for genuine authority, and actual need for restoration that constitute the reader's experience at any given moment of encounter.

The reader who brings their experience of institutional authority's failure to Mark's portrait of the scribes and Pharisees will find something that the reader who reads it only as historical narrative cannot access. The reader who brings their experience of genuine failure of discipleship to Peter's denial and flight will find something that the reader who reads it only as biography cannot find. The reader who brings their experience of the specific cost that faithfulness is currently demanding to the passion prediction cycles will find the teaching those cycles contain addressing them with a specificity that a more distanced reading would miss entirely. The text meets the reader where they actually are, and the depth of the meeting is proportional to the honesty with which the reader brings their actual situation rather than their idealized version of it.

The Permanent Invitation

The invitation that Mark extends — *come, follow me* — is the same invitation it extends to every reader who encounters it in every subsequent generation. It is addressed to people who do not fully understand what they are agreeing to, who will misunderstand the passion predictions, who will argue about greatness on the way to Jerusalem, who will fall asleep in Gethsemane, who will flee at the arrest, who will deny three times in the courtyard of the high priest, and who will need to receive the specific, named, unearned restoration of the resurrection message before they are capable of the faithfulness the call originally required. The invitation is not conditioned on the capacity to follow adequately. It is conditioned only on the willingness to follow at all — to leave the nets and the booth and the father in the boat and go in the direction the call specifies, knowing that the formation the call requires will happen through the following rather than before it, through the failure and restoration that Mark describes rather than in spite of them.

Mark was not written to produce people who have understood the Gospel completely and are living it out with consistent adequacy and without the failures that the disciples so honestly display. It was written to produce people who are in motion — who have heard the call, who have left something behind in response to it, who are discovering along the way that the urgency of the call is matched by the adequacy of the one who issued it to every condition that the following produces. For readers who bring to Mark the honest and sustained engagement it deserves, the most important thing the Gospel contains is not the sophistication of its Christological argument or the literary achievement of its narrative architecture, but the specific, concrete, forward-moving promise of the resurrection message: *he has risen, he is going ahead of you, there you will see him, just as he told you.*

The one who called beside the sea is the one who rose from the tomb. The one who rose from the tomb is the one who goes ahead to Galilee. The one who goes ahead to Galilee is going ahead still — into every context where the Gospel is genuinely received, every community where the cross is genuinely taken up, every season of failure where the specific restoration is genuinely needed. Mark's Gospel ends where genuine faith always finds its beginning — not in its own understanding, not in the achievements of the community, not in the resolution of its most searching questions, but in the empty tomb and the instruction to go, and in the discovery made by every generation that has followed the instruction that the one who went ahead was already there.

The Bible for Modern Life Series

This book is part of **The Bible for Modern Life** series—an ongoing collection that explores the meaning, historical setting, and message of individual books of Scripture.

Each volume looks closely at the biblical text to help readers understand what it meant in its original context and how its truths still apply to life today.

The goal is simple: to help modern readers engage more deeply with the Bible—one book at a time.

— Samuel Whitaker

www.ingramcontent.com/pod-product-compliance
Lightning Source LLC
Chambersburg PA
CBHW021328060726

47591CB00006B/1922